65 WISDOM PRINCIPLES

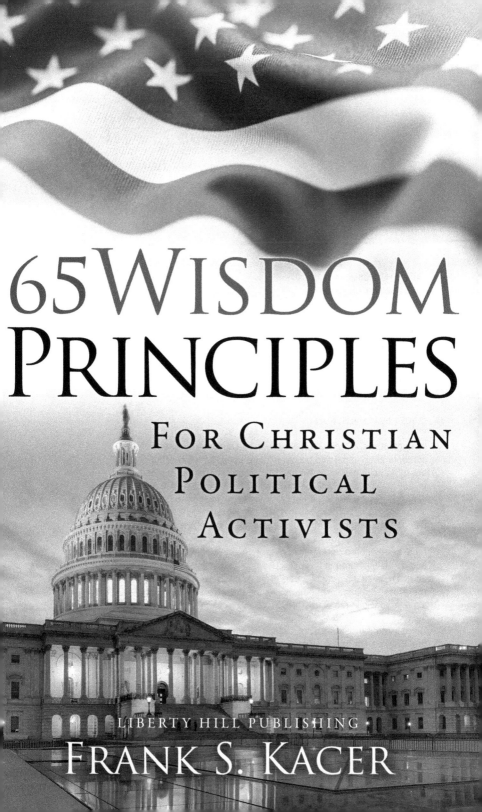

65 WISDOM PRINCIPLES

PRINCIPLES

FOR CHRISTIAN
POLITICAL
ACTIVISTS

LIBERTY HILL PUBLISHING

FRANK S. KACER

Liberty Hill Publishing
2301 Lucien Way #415
Maitland, FL 32751
407.339.4217
www.libertyhillpublishing.com

Unless otherwise indicated, Scripture quotations taken from
the English Standard Version (ESV). Copyright © 2001 by
Crossway, a publishing ministry of Good News Publishers. Used
by permission. All rights reserved.

Paperback ISBN-13: 978-1-6628-3803-3
Ebook ISBN-13: 978-1-6628-3804-0

FORWARD

T he apostle James tells us in **James 1:2** to "Count it all joy, my brothers, when you meet trials of various kinds, for you know that the testing of your faith produces steadfastness."

Christian, if you are going to get involved in politics, you will fall (or be pushed) into various trials, temptations, and opportunities to compromise your values. When this happens, we must remember that we do not get to respond as the world responds, according to our old human nature. We who belong to Christ are required to respond according to the nature of Christ that dwells within us to fulfill the purposes of the gospel, and ultimately to bring glory to our God.

The Bible is full of "imperatives" on how we should respond to the difficulties we face in the everyday world; that includes those circumstances that Christians face when they engage in the political battles of the day. An example is **Romans 12:17-21**: "Repay no one evil for evil, but give thought to do what is honorable in the sight of all. If possible, so far as it depends on you, live peaceably with all. Beloved, never avenge yourselves, but leave it to the wrath of god, for it is written, 'Vengeance is mine, I will repay, says the Lord.' To the contrary, 'if your enemy is hungry, feed him; if he is thirsty, give him something to drink; for by so doing you will heap burning coals on his head.' Do not be overcome by evil, but overcome evil with good."

In this book, Frank Kacer has captured the unique challenges that Christians face in trying to live a Christ-honoring life in the dynamic, and temptation-filled arena of politics. Frank provides an exceptional blending of political experience, relevant biblical principles and the mentoring heart of a pastor. The principles he has mined over many years of "Christian activism" are ones we can live by, not just in our political life but in everyday life as well.

Political engagement can manifest itself in many ways: elected office, campaign staff or volunteer, staff to elected officials, and part of the governmental bureaucracy itself. It's easy for Christians to overlook the importance of this last position, but we need honest, hardworking Christians literally every facet of government also.

In my over 20 years in elected office, I have personally had the opportunity to test the principles Frank has so carefully and insightfully identified and written about in "65 Principles." I can assure you that it's not easy to follow all of these, everyday. But I can also assure you that they all apply, everyday! My wife, family and I look at political service as a natural extension of our ministry service. For me, that service began as an associate pastor, then as a city councilman, then a state assemblyman and now as a state senator.

When you are in the tough arena of politics, and determine to play by God's rules, the world is going to press against you. You'll be challenged, your faith will be tested, your testimony will be tried, and your integrity and motives may be questioned. Whether you are a novice or an "old hand" in political service this outstanding book will help provide the focus you'll need as you're reminded whom you ultimately serve, your Lord and Savior Jesus Christ.

Finally, in your political pursuits, I encourage you to remember **Matthew 5:11-12:** "Blessed are you when others revile you and persecute you and utter all kinds of evil against you falsely on my account. Rejoice and be glad, for your reward is great in heaven." Rejoice and be glad! Keeping that perspective, and embracing the principles so well summarized in this book, will go a long way to sustaining you for the spiritual battles you will for certain encounter.

- Brian W. Jones, California State Senator

PREFACE

*"Righteousness exalts a nation,
but sin is a reproach to any people"*

Y ou can't escape politics; it's in the air you breathe. Politics is all over social media and in the news, it may be dividing your family, it can alienate you from your friends and neighbors, it can affect your job, and it's seriously dividing our nation.

As a Christian, you know something is gravely wrong with our government and the political environment that's systemic to it, so you want to do something, anything, to make a difference.

You've been taught that "true" change can only come about by changing hearts with the gospel of Jesus Christ (**Romans 10:9-17**). That statement is clearly true concerning a person's relationship to God, but it ignores the historical reality that Christians also impact culture, societies, and entire nations (including governments) by showing compassion to those that are oppressed (**Matthew 22:39**) and being salt and light (**Matthew 5:13-16**) everywhere, including in the political realm.

Being politically active can be exhilarating, but it's not for the faint-hearted. In a real sense political warfare mirrors the spiritual warfare around us. If you have an interest in politics, have dabbled in politics, have a desire to seek elective office, or are serving in elective office you already have an idea of the personal and professional cost involved.

That may be why many Christians complain about the government but won't get involved personally. It may also be why so many churches ignore teaching their members to be mature, discerning, and involved in "political" matters because that's "of the world" (**John 17:16**). However, I can assure you that ignoring the opportunity to provide godly political involvement is both unbiblical and unwise. In fact, without a godly presence to restrain governments, the Body of Christ's future ability to pursue its biblical mandates will become that much harder as the government assumes evermore "godlike" control over everything.

So, to help you on your political journey as a Christian, this booklet summarizes 65 "wisdom" principles to guide you no matter how involved you eventually become. They are intended to help you: vote, influence legislation, support an election campaign, advise those in elective office or any other position of influence, or even seek and serve in elective office yourself.

As you read, remember that the nature of politics almost guarantees everyone will have an opinion based on experience, the evening's news, the last book they read, or an eye-opening podcast someone shared. No one will agree with everything written here, but everyone from novice to seasoned warrior will find something of personal value.

A few final notes before you begin:

- This booklet is <u>not</u> a partisan political campaign training manual or a list of election requirements (e.g., candidate qualifications, financial reporting, or legal limitations). There are fine training camps and instructional materials available to the reader elsewhere.
- Wisdom principles are just that; principles. They are generally true, but there may be exceptions.
- Each chapter is self-contained, so jump around from principle to principle as much as you like.
- The English Standard Version (ESV) is used when Bible verses are cited. Those cited are for illustration only, in light of the rest of Scripture, and are intended to be a general, not a singular, authoritative understanding of that passage.

With that said, may the Lord bless your "political" journey and your activism far beyond your expectations (**Ephesians 3:20**).

ACKNOWLEDGMENTS

It's with deep gratitude that I dedicate this book to Lynn, my loving, godly wife of 48 years. Not only has she been patient during the many hours required to develop and write this material, but she has been a constant source of encouragement as I try to equip Christians for political battles for the sake of the gospel. Thank you honey; and thank you for being a Proverbs 31 woman by my side.

I would also like to thank Penny Harrington, David Daubenspeck, Don Cole and Pastor Tom Maxham for reviewing drafts of this book and providing much needed suggestions and corrections. Without their help, this book would have fallen far below where it is today.

TABLE OF CONTENTS

PART 1:

THE NARROW PATH INCLUDES THE POLITICAL

As a Christian, following the "narrow path" rightfully includes living a Christ-honoring life in everything we say and do. Although it isn't uncommon to think of kingdom work as only ministry within the church, or works of compassion to those that are suffering in the world, it also includes being salt and light in every legitimate activity we put our hearts and minds to. Not surprisingly then, engaging in politics is not "off limits" for us if we do it in a biblically grounded way. Said another way, we don't stop being a Christian when we dabble or energetically engage in the political realm. But be warned, activism in this area does provide some very unique challenges as well as opportunities.

Principle #1
Christians And Politics Actually Do Mix

"All Scripture is breathed out by God and profitable for teaching,
for reproof, for correction, and for training in righteousness,
that the man of God may be competent,
equipped for every good work"
2 Timothy 3:16-17

The world will always question the relevancy of Christianity for the issues of the "real world." The political left (progressives, mainstream news and entertainment, public education) in particular, but not exclusively, seem to have regard for Christians only when they can be manipulated to support secularist goals.

Apparently, anything beyond that usefulness should stay hidden behind chapel walls. In fact, much of the unbelieving world questions whether "religion" (read that as Christianity) should have any special legal protection or even respect since it's claimed we're all inherently racist, homophobic, ignorant, patriarchal, sexist, and mindlessly cling to discredited myths with a puritanical narrowness. To believe them, the Bible is not the solution, but is probably the root cause of most systemic and enduring problems.

As a Christian, it should be no surprise to you that spiritual darkness hates light, and you're a representative of God's light (**1 John 1:5-7**). But you also know that God is sovereign over everything, and "everything" includes politics (**Psalm 24:1**). And not only that, but you know God's eternal Word is not only sufficient for all matters of faith, but is applicable to everything relating to mankind's common good (**Deuteronomy 4:6-8; Proverbs 14:34**). The contrast, therefore, between darkness and light is that the world and its political philosophies are ultimately about death (**Romans 6:23a**), but God's Word is ultimately about the gospel, and life, and eternal life (**John 3:16; 14:6; Romans 6:23b**).

Second Timothy 3:16-17 says Scripture can make you competent for "every" good work. Since believers are uniquely gifted to understand God's truths (**1 Corinthians 2:14**), it would then seem that every "legitimate" human endeavor is ripe for Christian involvement and influence. More specifically, since Scripture doesn't condemn politics or political engagement per se (ignore heart issues for a moment), then it makes sense that political involvement can be a useful way (a tool) to promote good. After all, politics isn't intrinsically evil; its very essence is the art of negotiation and clear-conscience compromise to achieve a common good and to implement justice that is impartial.

That being said, does this mean every aspect of governmental power, influence, and involvement is spelled out biblically? Of course not! But it does imply a principled, moral foundation (i.e., a biblical worldview) can be used to evaluate and judge all decisions and actions, whether made by the political left or right. It also means that wisdom is needed to grapple with the complexities of exercising power. For you personally, it affects how you will run for elective office, which candidate you should support, what proposed laws are just, what duties the government should be focused on, how governmental power should be exercised domestically and abroad, etc., etc.

Governments will reflect the values of the people that wield its power, and the values of those that placed them into power through elections or appointments. If Christian values are withheld or removed anywhere along the line, disaster will inevitably follow as things begin to crumble (**Proverbs 29:2**).

It makes sense that Christians should be involved in politics at all levels, influencing what government does or doesn't do. If we don't restrain and properly direct governmental power, that power *will* eventually be abused by those that reject our values and our God.

PRINCIPLE #2
FOR EVERY MORAL ISSUE THERE'S A BIBLICAL REMEDY

---

*"Do not swerve to the right or to the left;
turn your foot away from evil"*
Proverbs 4:27

I s Scripture, specifically both the Old and New Testaments of the Bible, applicable to the contemporary problems our nation and our government faces today? The short answer is "Yes."

Why wouldn't God's Word apply? The same God that doesn't change (**Hebrews 13:8; James 1:17**), that created the entire universe and everything in it (**Genesis 1:1**), that sustains the universe by His will (**Hebrews 1:3**) is the same God that gave His people His everlasting, perfect Word (**Psalm 18:30; 119:89; Isaiah 40:8**). And that Word applies to all of life (**Psalm 119:11**) and the good works you are to do in this life (**Ephesians 2:8-10**).

The question is: are you willing to accept God's answers for the questions of the day, or are you going to chose to be a political pragmatist to promote yourself, or your favorite candidate, or embrace a purely secular (worldly wisdom) approach to solving our nation's problems?

God isn't too kind towards those that swing back and forth picking what's convenient from God's truth (cherry-picking), and then ignoring the "hard stuff" while embracing more popular, worldly solutions to contemporary problems (**James 1:5-8**). If that describes you, you better seriously consider what it means for you to be a Christian. Consider yourself warned, you can't serve two masters, politics and Christ, because only one will be dominant (**Matthew 6:24**).

Now, relying on God's Word doesn't mean there's always a clear statement in Scripture that readily answers all your questions. Many principles are germane to any complex issue, and wisdom is necessary to decide which to apply and when. Take the example of illegal immigration. The Bible has much to say about justice (**Leviticus 19:15; Proverbs 21:15**) and the rule of law (**1 Timothy 1:8-11**), compassion and mercy (**Matthew 22:39**), maintaining order (**Romans 13:1-4; 1 Corinthians 14:33**), how to treat foreigners (**Exodus 12:49**), and even family protection and security (**Exodus 22:2-3**). These are just a sample of the principles that could apply, with each facet needing to be considered when practical solutions are eventually proposed.

God knows us all well. He's not surprised by the modern-day problems that plague our cities, states, and nation. And, He has given us His eternal Word to help us through this life and to navigate how to handle every moral problem we face, whether it's labeled as political or not. Ultimately, however, the right approach (or approaches) to any problem must be what will honor the Lord and be consistent with His character.

The bottom line is that experts and professionals may know how to implement specific policies to maximize return on investment, but they may not be the best source of guiding principles that any practical problem solution should conform to. Without those godly values providing the foundation, the solution will eventually become what's best for those in authority that are wielding decision power.

God specializes in knowing the human heart (**Jeremiah 17:9; 2 Corinthians 5:17**), and gives us His standard to be the best judge of what's right or wrong. Since every political issue has a moral component to it, God's Word will always be applicable. But beware; it may take some real digging and research to find that right solution.

PRINCIPLE #3

STRIVE FOR A BIBLICAL BALANCE OF ZEAL AND KNOWLEDGE

"I bear witness that they have a zeal for God,
but not according to knowledge"
Romans 10:2

Our society looks favorably on "Type A's" because they accomplish so much. On one hand it shows a passion for life, achievement, and excellence. On the other hand, sheer accomplishment can easily distract you from taking time to be deeply immersed in the things of God.

In the realm of Christians and politics, there are two very common extremes of Type A's.

One group ignores their duty to be godly citizens, and plunge themselves into energetic biblical studies, attending every available Sunday school class and seminar, and spending countless hours researching the latest "new wrinkle" on some esoteric theological point. Don't get me wrong, it's good to be captivated by God's Word (**Psalm 119:15**) but not as an excuse to ignore one of our key imperatives: to be salt and light to the world (**Matthew 5:13-16**). This oversight can come perilously close to not living the very truth you are to seek to understand (**2 Timothy 3:7**).

The other extreme Type A group sees our government embracing self-destructive values and they want to do everything possible to reverse this trend for the good of their families and the cause of Christ. These believers can easily get caught up in political tactics, intrigue, and power plays, and can develop a condescending attitude towards Christians that may be less sensitive to the politically-charged spiritual war around us. These zealots, contrary to Scripture, may even wrap the flag around their Bible and see them as almost one and the same: God and country forever! Although patriotic, they can easily assume the weight of this battle on their shoulders and forget how to rest in the loving hands of an all-powerful God in whom we are to put our trust (**Proverbs 3:5**).

Unfortunately, there are also many Christians that may see the danger around them, but they're perfectly content to be a bystander, watching the ongoing political circus with sarcasm and skepticism. If you fall into this category, be careful, because you may be inadvertently contributing to the problem instead of responsibly working to help further God's kingdom (**Revelation 3:15-16**).

You know that too much study can weary the soul (**Ecclesiastes 12:12**) and lack of zeal for the things of God is not good (**Romans 12:11**). You also know faith without works is dead (**James 2:17**) and zeal without knowledge can become prideful (**Proverbs 19:2; Romans 10:2-3**). So how do you get that sweet spot of disciplined balance?

First, constantly seek the Lord's will in everything you do to ensure your decisions: glorify Him (**1 Corinthians 10:31**), build unity with other believers (**Ephesians 4:3**), show charity towards others, and prevent you from overlooking your personal and family responsibilities (**1 Timothy 5:8**).

Second, immerse yourself in God's Word (**Psalm 1:1-2**) while studying the issues of the day. This will be critical to equip you for political battle. It will also remind you of your dual citizenship, both here and in heaven (**Philippians 3:20**); and that the Lord is sovereign, not you (**Job 42:2; Psalm 115:3**).

Finally, allow yourself to be accountable to a mature believer who will challenge you in your personal life and how you are handling your priorities. Maintaining balance is going to be hard work, but it can be done with the Lord's help if you remain teachable and open to advice (**Proverbs 12:1; 13:18**).

Principle #4
Apply Biblical Truth With Caution

"I have applied all these things to myself and Apollos
for your benefit, brothers, that you may learn by us not to
go beyond what is written, that none of you may be puffed up
in favor of one against another"
1 Corinthians 4:6

While living in a fallen world, one of the more difficult challenges that Christians face is applying biblical truths to secular (specifically governmental) activities in a Christ-honoring way. It may seem easy, but mining helpful governance insights while being faithful to the meaning and intent of any scriptural text can be daunting. It's easy to do an internet word or topical search, take a verse out of context, and then apply it in some preconceived manner to "prove" a point with "biblical authority" behind it.

To the theologically trained this "cavalier" approach is akin to heresy. To those Christians that are biblically ignorant this is a readily accepted, authoritative justification for their position. For liberal Christians it is appropriating "outdated biblical guidance" for a misguided authoritative application. To a relative few, however, it's a valid attempt to glean general scriptural principles to determine if a policy under scrutiny either violates or is consistent with general truth.

That latter approach above will generally appeal to both common sense and experience. The obvious difficulty that can occur for general applications is when different principles pulled from different texts may appear to contradict each other. When that happens, usually more research and study will make the application clearer. An example is the prohibition against taking life (**Exodus 20:13**) and the use of capital punishment

(**Genesis 9:6**). The principle that clarifies both has to do with fulfilling the need for justice (**Romans 13:1-4**).

A good rule of thumb when trying to find a scriptural basis for a political position is: the further the application is away from clear biblical commands, the more caution and wisdom are needed in its application.

The reality is that once we get past "thou shalt" or "thou shalt not" types of clear biblical statements, we increase the risk of using a biblical text wrongly. In fact, as the application becomes more tenuous, that's the time we need to be more gracious towards each other and work more diligently to prevent any unintended divisiveness that can easily develop. This is hard enough to do in explicitly Christian circles; it's even more difficult to do in highly-charged political battles where an issue may have many principles to be considered, and practical tradeoffs need to be weighed.

Another important concern is that different Christians may have different levels of conviction concerning the specific use of biblical principles. Some Christians may concur with the direct application, while others may agree with the principle but allow for some softening when applied to a current decision. The real issue may become a need for compromise on near-term tactics to gain ground on achieving godly long-term goals. This is where believers need to be gracious (and realistic) with each other (**Colossians 3:12-14**) while maintaining a clear conscience.

The bottom line is that there are biblical truths, principles, historical examples, wisdom, and insights that can be applied to the myriad political issues of our day. Scripture is sufficient for all matters of faith (**Hebrews 11:1-3**) and practice (**Psalm 119:105**); and practice can include fighting for public policy that aligns with biblical insights and is intended for the common good (**2 Timothy 3:16-17**).

You will quickly find that working through the application of Scripture for any political issue will be challenging, frustrating, and rewarding, all at the same time. But I can guarantee you, it'll be worth the effort.

PRINCIPLE #5

THERE'S NO SUCH THING AS PEACEFUL CO-EXISTENCE WITH POLITICAL DARKNESS

*"Your adversary the devil prowls around like a roaring lion,
seeking someone to devour. Resist him, firm in your faith,
knowing that the same kinds of suffering are being experienced by
your brotherhood throughout the world"*
1 Peter 5:8-9

Reaching across the political aisle is a noble-sounding phrase conveying the idea we can all work together for the common good. This usually happens when a clear and present danger threatens our nation (e.g., terrorist attacks, war, true pandemics, major natural disasters, etc.).

The problem with this political "reach" is that cooperation is possible only when there are shared principles or moral values. When there was a more dominant Christian underpinning to our society, common ground was far more common. Today's political divide is more than just differences of opinion on how to best care for people and protect our liberties (restrained by virtue!). It is a clash of different worldviews: one a reflection of life and accountability to a Creator (**Job 33:4; Ecclesiastes 12:13-14**), the other a secular belief system that sees man as the ultimate determiner and controller of everything (**Psalm 53:1**).

To think there's some "moral equivalency" between these two views of existence is not just naïve, it's dangerous. Any ideological framework that enshrines man's wisdom above God's wisdom is doomed to failure. For example, a political ideology that embraces ungodly abortion on demand, has normalized sexual perversion, assumes responsibility to "educate" everyone's child, believes a government should be led by elitists that know better how society should function, is fundamentally incompatible with the values of a biblical worldview.

Obviously, there are "good" people all along the political spectrum that mean well. But those that embrace destructive secular theologies out of a Pollyanna view of life are just useful tools for the evil one to "innocently" stoke hatred and death (**1 Peter 5:8-9**). Recognizing this huge political (and ideological) divide, it's no wonder political compromise has become so rare; evil will never give back what it thinks it owns. In fact, a political ideology that is man-centered and confident of its goodness will demonize, threaten, disparage, misrepresent, accuse, slander, and ultimately try to eradicate (read that as destroy) any opposition. That's what evil is, that's what evil does (**John 8:44**), and, it is unrelenting!

As a result, our nation's political battles are no longer a tit-for-tat exercise in responsible compromise in governance. Public political discourse emanating from a secular, broken worldview is now more akin to the entrapment that comes with smooth talk that ends in death (**Proverbs 5:1-6**).

What should be done, given this politically uncomfortable reality? First, wickedness needs to be exposed for what it is, and those actions and decisions that contribute to the furtherance of evil should be roundly condemned (**Ephesians 5:11**). Ignoring this responsibility will only strengthen the hand of those that hate our values.

Secondly, an articulate defense and promotion of biblically sound principles needs to be offered up at every opportunity. This needs to be done without being embarrassed or intimidated for standing by your convictions (**1 Peter 3:13-17**), or acknowledging the source of those convictions (**Matthew 10:32-33**).

Make no mistake about it, this is a war. But with any war involving kingdom work, you can be confident because you're a soldier in the army of the living God, and He will ultimately prevail (**Ephesians 6:10-20**).

PRINCIPLE #6

POLITICS TO THE FAR RIGHT, OR THE FAR LEFT, OF A BIBLICAL WORLDVIEW WILL EVENTUALLY BE DISASTROUS

"Do not swerve to the right or to the left;
turn your foot away from evil"
Proverbs 4:27

Politically, the left is fond of portraying anything conservative as being far right, extremist, on the wrong side of history, or just plain out-of-touch. In other words, conservative views are destructive to everyone and everything, while the left's positions are noble, reasonable, and commonsense. The reality is that when conservative beliefs are aligned with God's truths and principles they are "middle-of-the-road" and profoundly effective, while both leftist and far-right views are extreme.

To gain political power, the left purposely embraces two errors. The first is an unwillingness to recognize and accept the reality of the consequences of their policies and laws. Using "feel good," great-sounding slogans that are clearly destructive when implemented is a form of prideful blindness that is both unmerited and unjustifiable, and needs to be exposed (**Proverbs 10:14; 18:12; Ephesians 5:11**).

The second error is not accepting that there are true "far-right" positions that are destructive; and that those positions are not conservative or biblical. A case in point is the issue of life. The far left arbitrarily gives or takes away value concerning life based on circumstances. Hence, abortion is a mother's right, capital punishment is premeditated murder by the government, physician-assisted suicide is a personal freedom, and embryos are expendable for science purposes no matter how improbable any scientific success will be.

The actual (radical) far right position treats life as if it were virtually divine and needs to be protected at all costs, whether it's a baby inside the mother, a mass murderer, or someone struggling with terminal cancer that will consume every ounce of resource available to extend their life even if it involves cryogenically freezing themselves far into the future.

The conservative, biblical position about life is founded on justice: it's unjust to kill an innocent child, it's just to take the life of one who murders other innocent life, and it's just (and compassionate) to comfort and sustain someone who's dying until death occurs naturally (**Matthew 22:39**). This "middle," reasonable, position recognizes the worth of life that is created in God's image (**Genesis 1:27**), that it deserves to be protected (**Exodus 20:13**), but that it's not sacrosanct (**Genesis 9:6**).

The same reframing of the political spectrum can be done for any major issue. Consider the nature of the environment: the far left treats it as effectively divine, the far right sees it purely in a utilitarian way, but the biblical view revolves around stewardship. What about the role of the government? The far left sees it as a tool to exercise absolute control of everything, the far right sees it in terms of a theocracy, but the Bible emphasizes its role to exercise justice and commend what's good. One more example: gun ownership. The far left thinks only the government should have weapons, the far right sees personal ownership of any level of lethality as fine, but biblically both the government and individuals are justified to have weapons for defensive purposes.

The bottom line, therefore, is that if you want to be an effective influencer (**Matthew 5:13-16**), you need to work through the implications of properly framing the issues of the day (**Ecclesiastes 7:27**) and not allowing others to define your values as the extreme position. By properly reframing the argument you lay the groundwork for properly defending biblical truth in practical ways that the average person can understand (**2 Timothy 2:15-16**). And, it will simultaneously expose any irrational hatred for all things conservative (**John 3:20; 15:18**).

Part 2:
Ultimate Matters
Really Do Matter

H ow you will spend your eternity is based solely on your personal relationship to Jesus Christ through faith in His sacrificial death on the cross and resurrection. Keeping that perspective will have a great impact on your attitude towards political involvement in this world. Politics is important, but it should never be allowed to become an idol that captures your ultimate affections. Honoring the Lord in everything you do should be the measure of your life, not the number of elections that are won.

PRINCIPLE #7

YOUR ETERNAL SALVATION ISN'T DEPENDENT ON YOUR POLITICS

*"For by grace you have been saved through faith.
And this is not your own doing; it is the gift of God,
not a result of works, so that no one may boast"*
Ephesians 2:8-9

It's exhilarating to fight for a cause that's just, or for a godly candidate willing to stand in public for what's right. There's going to be joy and discouragement in all your political pursuits, and oftentimes you're going to be forced to deeply reflect on what happened after a particularly difficult battle.

These ups and downs are part of life, and should be expected since you don't know the future, and ultimately you have little control over outcomes. But whether there's been a devastating political loss or not, you know there will be many more battles ahead. And, no matter how important the fight, no matter how devastating the consequences of an election defeat, your faith in Christ and your eternal salvation remain secure because your destiny depends upon what Christ did and not how many votes were won (**John 6:37; 14:6**).

On the other hand, you could win every election, defeat every political foe, be an advisor to the President, and even conquer the world; but if you're not a believer then everything you've gained is worthless, a mere chasing after the wind (**Mark 8:36**).

Political battles are a reflection of the ongoing spiritual battles across our nation. You know these battles will continue until the Lord returns in triumph to establish His eternal kingdom (**1 Thessalonians 4:16-18**). But until then, you're to be faithful and enthusiastic in the fights around you, and be a warrior that stands for righteousness until the end (**2 Timothy 4:7**). If you are doing battle for the glory of God, you can do this with confidence and a clear conscience, knowing your relationship to God and your eternal dwelling place are secure today and forevermore because of the work of Jesus Christ (**Romans 6:10**).

That truth is transcendent and not dependent on how well you ran a campaign, or whether abortion is finally abolished. Those are important battles, but your personal example of what it means to be a Christian, to be indwelt with the Holy Spirit (**Ephesians 1:11-14**), and to live out being salt and light in the political realm (**Matthew 5:13-16**) is what will bring glory to God (**1 Corinthians 10:31**).

You are interested in politics because you know politics is an extremely important and difficult battlefield. You want to do the best you can because you know the results may have a profound impact on many other lives. You may even believe that political battle is your calling in this life and is more important than any other career you could pursue.

But, with that fervor you need to be extremely careful you don't equate your worth with some political outcome. Ultimately, your value to God is based on what Jesus Christ has done to secure your salvation and make you part of His kingdom (**Philippians 3:20**) and His family (**Ephesians 1:5**). Knowing and constantly remembering that truth should encourage you to continue the good fight, knowing the war belongs to the Lord, and that the ultimate victory is assured (**1 John 5:4-5**), whether there are some setbacks in this life or not.

Finally, keep in mind that when you ultimately face the Lord, He won't be asking you which political party you were registered with, or whether Assembly Bill 735 was passed or not, or even if you won more elections than you lost. These have nothing to do with eternal life (**Ephesians 2:8-9**). Instead, you will want to hear Him simply say "well done, good and faithful servant" (**Matthew 25:21**).

BELIEVERS SHARE MORE IN COMMON THROUGH JESUS CHRIST THAN THEY EVER WILL IN POLITICS

"No, in all these things we are more than conquerors through him who loved us. For I am sure that neither death nor life, nor angels nor rulers, nor things present nor things to come, nor powers, nor height nor depth, nor anything else in all creation, will be able to separate us from the love of God in Christ Jesus our Lord"
Romans 8:37-39

For a Christian, politics can become a modern-day crusade of sorts, the equivalent of a "non-violent" holy war. Because biblical values are at stake, and you have a sincere desire to honor the Lord, there's a high potential to become "religiously" strident in whatever position you take on important issues, or who the best candidate should be.

If you develop this "self-rightness" attitude, it will undoubtedly affect your relationship with other believers that are just as committed as you are to improving our city, county and nation. And if that's true with those that are dedicated and knowledgeable, think about the potential for conflict when there are substantive differences in points of view.

But before you start to judge the motives or commitment of others, remember two things.

The first is that you're nothing without Christ (**John 14:6; 15:5; Philippians 4:13,19**). Without Him, you're lost and without hope in everything you do. If Christ had not become the Lord over your life, anything you try to do would be just filthy rags (**Isaiah 64:6; Philippians 3:8-9**), no matter how "right" you thought you were. The fact that you belong to God means that everything you do now is to honor Him. But besides doing the right thing, you also need to do it the right way. If you acknowledge the Lord is the One that has given you political insights, motivation, and understanding, you should be humbled and not entertain any opportunity to become puffed up with pride (**1 Corinthians 8:1-2**).

The second thing to remember is that when you have disagreements with other believers, those brothers and sisters are just as important to God as you are! Any "light and momentary" political differences you may be having are nothing compared to what you share in common.

Consider these facts. You are both: created in God's image and likeness (**Genesis 1:26-27**), created for good works (**Ephesians 2:10**), chosen by God before the foundation of the world (**Ephesians 1:4**), given eternal life (**Matthew 25:46; John 3:16**), indwelt with the Holy Spirit (**1 Corinthians 2:12**), are gifted by God (**1 Corinthians 12:4-7**), heard by God the Father in your prayers (**1 Peter 3:12a**), God's ambassadors (**2 Corinthians 5:20**), and are both co-heirs with Christ (**Romans 8:17**).

So, what's more important to you, winning a small, temporary political skirmish, or doing everything you can to build each other up in your mutual work to honor the Lord? This doesn't mean differences shouldn't be worked out; but it does mean that you are to hold those in God's family in high regard, value and love them, and cherish your mutual love for God.

Differences will occur, conflicts can become heated, mistakes will be made, elections will be won and lost, but brothers and sisters in Christ are family (**John 1:12; Ephesians 2:19; 1 John 3:1**). And that family relationship will exist into eternity because of what Christ has done for you, not as a result of any campaign or election; and definitely not as a result of having some uniformly agreed to political orthodoxy.

Principle #9

Why Are You Involved In Politics?

"But seek first the kingdom of God and his righteousness, and all these things will be added to you"
Matthew 6:33

This is a pop quiz for you: why are you involved in politics?

Is it an altruistic belief you can "change the world"? Is it your desire to be a good citizen and exercise your freedom to influence the government? Do you think you're specially gifted in politics and want to use your abilities for God's glory? Are others encouraging you to engage because they think you're able to make a difference? Do you have a friend running for elective office that is in need of your help? Or, do you think you're "called by God" to eventually run for office yourself and see this as a Good Samaritan type of ministry in a dark place?

None of these reasons are necessarily bad unless your motivation is purely to feed your pride (**1 John 2:15-16**). Hopefully, that temptation is not the case! But if it is, you better spend some serious time in prayer and seeking counsel from mature believers.

For a believer, political warfare is a manifestation of real-life spiritual warfare. Like all wars, there are two opposing sides, two different worldviews in play, two different commanders, and numerous battles. But since it has spiritual roots, we know what the ultimate means and ends are of the enemy: to blind the minds of unbelievers (**Luke 8:12; 2 Corinthians 4:4**), to promote false truths (**Galatians 1:6-9**), to deceive (**2 Corinthians 11:3**), and to destroy as many lives as possible (**1 Peter 5:8**). One sure-fire way to do this is to destroy the ability (or remove the opportunity) to proclaim the gospel – the only true help and hope there is for a fallen world.

Political tools play heavily in the ongoing cosmic battle. Raw governmental power can be used to remove hindrances to the proclamation of the gospel, or it can be used to make it extremely difficult. It can be used to declare what's evil as being good, and what's good as being evil (**Isaiah 5:20-21**). The same duality is true for the general principles in Scripture that are intended for mankind's good. When these principles are followed, blessings result, when they're ignored disastrous consequences will predictably follow (**Deuteronomy 28:1-67; Proverbs 14:34**).

As a Christian, you should be constantly evaluating the impact any particular law, policy, ordinance, and even candidate will have on the promotion or suppression of God's truths, particularly the proclamation of the gospel. This will take a lot of hard work and wisdom in working through what may not always be obvious implications. But it will be rewarding work, and will keep God's honor and His intent for *your* political involvement at the forefront of your decisions.

You may be thinking that type of evaluation is a stretch, or that it over-spiritualizes everything. If you think that, then you're in effect saying God doesn't care about "politics" unless, maybe, resulting laws make it illegal for pastors to preach the gospel (**Acts 4:19-20; 5:29**). That's a very narrow view of God's provision through the government and His love for His creatures (**Numbers 11:23; Matthew 6:25-34**). After all, He is the Creator of this world and owns everything in it (**Genesis 1:1; Deuteronomy 10:14; Psalm 24:1**), and He has appointed you to be His salt-and-light representative (**Matthew 5:13-16**) in everything you do, and that includes political ministry.

The bottom line is that if your involvement in politics is to honor you, your efforts will be no better than the Pharisees (**Matthew 23:1-12**) of old that were self-righteous. If it is to honor the Lord, then your focus will be to fight for what's right in God's eyes, and not the eyes of anyone else (**1 Corinthians 10:31**).

Principle #10

Elections Give Us What We Need, And What The Nation Deserves

"And the Lord said to Samuel, 'Obey the voice of the people in all that they say to you, for they have not rejected you, but they have rejected me from being king over them'"
1 Samuel 8:7

In your quiet moments, have you ever seriously considered what you and the rest of the body of Christ need? You know the Lord has promised to meet your daily necessities of life (**Matthew 6:25-34**), but He also promises to mature you for your good and to become a better reflection of His glory (**Hebrews 12:5-11**). How does He do this? God does this more often than not by bringing uncomfortable situations into your life to challenge your faith (**1 Peter 4:12-17**). These trials will chastise, discipline, and yes, refine you.

So, what does this have to do with politics?

When a nation experiences relative calm politically, believers usually have a great opportunity to freely proclaim the gospel, reach out to those in need, and exemplify Christ in their lives without major interference. Kingdom work during those times, if taken seriously, can expand quickly and end up not just influencing the culture but also government leadership to do what is right and just (**Romans 13:1-4**). This will have a profound impact on an entire nation (**Proverbs 29:2a**). When that happens, governments can be encouraged to focus on their primary roles of executing justice and encouraging good instead of finding new ways to control people's lives (**Proverbs 14:34**).

However, if those opportune times of relative peace are squandered, then it's virtually inevitable that the political winds will change and worldviews hostile to Christian values will take over. The clear result will be a government more antagonistic to Christ-honoring spiritual growth. If this threat is only weakly challenged, or ignored entirely by the Christian community, hostility will inevitably grow until the Body of Christ is forced to take action to protect itself. Historically, that turning point begins with godly repentance (confessing complacency, apathy, and being worldly), and then a revival as the church returns to its high calling of kingdom building (**Jeremiah 29:7; Romans 12:2-3**) and speaking truth to power (**Luke 12:11-12**).

This process, though painful at the time, is needed to burn away any worthless "Christian chaff" (**Zechariah 13:9**) and make way for God's remnant to return to the basic imperatives of Scripture: influence, mercy, and evangelism (**Matthew 5:13-16; 22:39; 28:18-20**). Faithfully pursuing these mandates will eventually result in positive change (**Matthew 16:18**) and the cycle (with its unique opportunities) begins all over again.

For any country, if it embraces biblical principles and godly justice it will prosper and be a testimony to the world of God's blessings (**Deuteronomy 28:1-14; Proverbs 14:34a**). But as a nation embraces ungodliness and promotes wickedness with impunity it is unknowingly inviting what it rightfully deserves: God's judgment (**Proverbs 29:2b**). After all, it is God that holds entire nations in His hands; He can raise one up to honor Him, and He can just as easily bring a wicked one down (**Job 12:23**).

The politically insightful Christian will understand the times they're living in and will recognize the opportunities available to glorify God through political engagement (**1 Chronicles 12:32**). This can happen no matter what part of the overall life cycle the nation, and God's self-identified church, is in.

23

Part 3:
Test Yourself First

D o you think you have your life in order and have everything figured out? Be careful, pride really does precede a fall. You need to test yourself in everything; particularly in your priorities and in those areas you think you are strong.

THE "RIGHTER" YOU ARE, THE "WRONGER" EVERYONE ELSE WILL APPEAR

"There are those who are clean in their own eyes
but are not washed of their filth"
Proverbs 30:12

Politics is invigorating. If you become passionate about particular candidates or are able to gain tremendous support for godly legislation, you're energized. Because each battle will become a microcosm of the larger, universal spiritual warfare, you'll begin to think of yourself as one of the Lord's warriors in the equivalent of a holy war.

You know ultimately that the battle is not against flesh and blood, but against the spiritual powers of darkness (**Ephesians 6:12**). So, it's natural that as you become more convinced of the "rightness" of your cause, and victories start to mount up, it becomes that much easier to de-humanize your opponents since they are obviously on the side of evil. If and when you do that, you have made a foolish error, you have forgotten that your opponents are made in the image of God, just like you (**Genesis 1:27**). Unfortunately, that mistake can lead to your conscious or unconscious refusal to give the level of respect your opponent deserves by being God's fellow image bearer.

Recognizing the humanity of those that actively reject your values doesn't mean you agree with your opponents, or that you need to defer to them or believe everything they say. In fact, you of all people, by knowing the worldview that probably forms most of their thinking should understand their natural blindness towards God's truths (**1 Corinthians 2:14**). However, that doesn't mean you stop setting a godly example concerning them (**Galatians 6:10**), or in how you pray for them (**Romans 10:1**), or even how you refer to them. Trying to set a Christ-like example will go a long way to being the witness to the world that you're called to be, even in the hotbed (or minefield) of political engagement. And, how you treat your opponents may even result in a level of mutual respect that will have a lasting impact on everyone around you (**1 Peter 3:13-17**).

But what about those "on your side" of the political aisle that don't fully agree with your positions or the election campaigns you're supporting? The more convinced you are of the purity of your political passion, the more anyone disagreeing with you will begin to look like the enemy (whether they are believers or not!). This is a terrible road to go down; particularly since there are so many more battles in the future that you will need support in fighting. Either you learn to work together now, or you will end up fighting the next battles alone.

So, do you think of yourself as the strong one and everyone else is weak and needs to follow your lead? Although you may have a hard time with those you think are the weaker brother or sister (**Romans 14:1,4**), remember that God says for you to always be charitable and gentle, and to try to build unity and stay clear of division (**Proverbs 15:1; 1 Corinthians 1:10; Ephesians 4:2; Colossians 3:12-14**). In fact, Scripture says for you to consider others better than yourself (**Philippians 2:3**). If you have a hard time doing that, read **Romans 12:3** over a few times.

Finally, remember that everything you have has been given to you by God (**James 1:17**). Also, there's nothing intrinsically good about you that would merit God showering His blessings on you (**Ephesians 2:8-9**) or any of your activities. This realization should create a humble spirit in you; particularly as you remember that those without Christ are first and foremost in desperate need of a Redeemer, while those that do know Christ have been adopted into the same family of God that you are part of (**John 1:9-13**).

PRINCIPLE #12

WE'RE ALWAYS ACCOUNTABLE FOR HOW WE HANDLE TRUTH

"Do your best to present yourself to God as one approved,
a worker who has no need to be ashamed,
rightly handling the word of truth"
2 Timothy 2:15

A well-turned phrase is a powerful tool to convey wisdom or get across an important concept or thought. The **Book of Proverbs** is an especially wealthy source of pithy statements that are short, insightful, and memorable. But like any authoritative statement, its context must be understood for its insights to be used effectively. Otherwise, you are only using God's Word as a pretext to prove something His Word was never intended to be used for.

As a Christian, you should know a lot of Scripture, and even be able to quote (or quickly look up) verses that are especially meaningful to you and useful to help you understand complex political issues. However, when using them to persuade others, they can easily be misapplied or legitimately challenged unless the verses are consistent with the rest of Scripture and also with objective reality (**Deuteronomy 5:33; 28:1-67; Proverbs 13:21**).

This booklet is a case in point. Scripture is used throughout, but its particular application to any given topic is only valid if it resonates consistently with the rest of the Bible. Many times, a scriptural principle can be applied to a broader slice of life (and politics) even though its original context was much narrower in application. This is not wrong to do, but it must be done with care. That being said, several points need to be amplified a bit.

First, don't go beyond what can be reasonably inferred or meant or illustrated by a verse. An example is saying that **Psalm 24:1** means Jesus Christ rules this world and earthly rulers have no say or power at all ("The earth is the LORD's and the fullness thereof, the world and those who dwell therein"). But the everyday reality is that earthly powers (both good and evil ones) are placed in authority by God over us for our good (**Romans 13:1-4**). We know that some time in the future, Jesus will directly rule the world when He returns in glory, but for now earthly authorities are serving His purposes and exercising incredible power.

Secondly, using Scripture must not contradict the rest of Scripture. Cults do this all the time by taking selected verses to try and prove a false doctrinal point. A classic example is saying Jesus is not divine by using **John 20:17**, while ignoring verses from the same gospel writer (**John 10:33**) that show people around Jesus clearly understood His claim to be God (obviously, many other verses also prove Jesus' divinity, e.g., **Colossians 1:15-20; Hebrews 1:1-3**; etc.). Likewise, taking verses completely out of context and glibly misusing them to support a political agenda is shameful and will only lead to ridicule (**2 Peter 3:16**)

Third, don't take an authoritative position based on an isolated verse that's difficult to understand or is obscure. Doing this will only create controversy and end up focusing attention on the applicability of that verse, instead of what Scripture has to offer in general concerning the topic at hand.

Finally, there may be competing principles from Scripture that will require wisdom to determine how they may best apply to a current situation. A case in point is what to do about people that have entered the country illegally. Should they be shown mercy and compassion (**Matthew 22:39; Luke 10:25-37**) or be immediately deported (**Ecclesiastes 8:11**)?

The more well-rounded you are in understanding key truths throughout Scripture the better equipped you'll be in "rightly handling the word of truth" (**2 Timothy 2:15**). Matching God's truths with your understanding of the practical aspects of key political issues will go a long way to ensure you don't come across as a religious simpleton instead of an effective influencer.

Principle #13
Beware Of Political Idolatry

"Do not be idolaters as some of them were"
1 Corinthians 10:7a

One of the saddest things to listen to is someone describing how they destroyed their marriage, angered their children, alienated their friends, and lost their job because their priorities weren't right. What they're really saying is that there was something that captured their passions so much that they put it ahead of everything else of importance, even as the rest of their life crumbled.

Political warfare, by its nature, is a never-ending battle. It's sometimes hotter than at other times, but it will continue to rage until the Lord returns. Politics is not like a nation going to war with another nation, where attention must be riveted in common-cause for survival for a period of years, and then it may come to an end. Politics is always adapting, but never really changing or ever actually finished. In many ways, once a person gets bitten by the political "bug" it's hard to ever be fully cured and be restored to some level of balanced health.

That's one of the challenges of politics: the illusive striving for a cause bigger than you that never has an end and that can take everything you have. For a Christian this is even more insidious since it's very tempting to cloak your passion for politics in biblical rationalizations. When that's done, who can argue with "God told me to do this?"

Before you say you have everything in balance, just know that many pastors (who of all people should know better) have shipwrecked their families by the same rationalizations concerning ministry (**1 Timothy 5:8**). It's the rare person that can keep balance and priorities right, but that has to be your constant goal. Otherwise, you are going to irreparably harm those that are dear to you, and bring dishonor on the very Lord you claim to be serving.

So how do you keep your political passion in check, and not allow it to become an idol of your heart?

First, remember that excessive passions that get in the way of honoring the Lord are temptations that everyone faces. Thankfully, the Lord promises to provide a way of relief if you're willing to seek it out (**1 Corinthians 10:13**). You may not like what you will need to do, but that is the real test: are you trying to please the Lord, or feed your pride?

Secondly, pray for help and wisdom. When you do, ask for what you need to hear and not what you want to hear. You'll have friends that want to be an encouragement to you, but they may not be as objective as you need (**Proverbs 27:14**). Also, you need to be careful what you pray for. Is your prayer "the Lord's will be done" or that your will must be done (**Proverbs 28:26; Matthew 6:10**)?

Third, you need to be accountable to trusted advisors that know you well and are willing to confront you if needed. In fact, these individuals need to be willing to question your spouse (if you are married) or anyone else that's close to you to find out what they think is actually going on in your life (**Proverbs 11:14; 12:15; 15:22; 19:20-21; 24:6; 27:5**).

It's one thing to take on a huge commitment for a short period of time – we all understand that. It's quite another to go from crises to crises, or campaign to campaign in the political realm in a never-ending drain of you as a person while taking those closest to you for granted. Scripture says that the prudent will see this type of danger and turn from it, but the simple will just continue on and suffer (**Proverbs 27:12**).

So, which do you want to be, the prudent one or the simpleton?

PRINCIPLE #14

ARE YOU WILLING TO TELL YOUR FAMILY THEY'RE #2 FOR A SEASON?

"But if anyone does not provide for his relatives, and especially for members of his household, he has denied the faith and is worse than an unbeliever"
1 Timothy 5:8

So maybe politics isn't an idol in your heart, but it is very important to you. Just remember, families and loved ones can put up with a lot if it's for a short period of time.

Probably everyone has had life circumstances when they're focused on some major crisis that prevented them from taking care of their normal family responsibilities. It could be a major job deadline or looking for a job, a medical emergency, studying for a career-changing certification, or anything else that takes incredible amounts of time, focus, and energy. The one redeeming aspect is when there's an end in sight; and that end is not decades away.

Political warfare is an unforgiving task master. If you let it, it will consume everything you have and then demand more. Whether you're running for office, supporting a candidate, or in a hot fight for some needed legislation: you can never do enough to ensure success. Realistically, there will always be more to be done than can be done.

During these high commitment times, you need to be brutally honest with your family. You may be reassuring them that you love them and that they're your highest priority, but your actions will probably tell a different story (**Romans 16:18**). What happens when media interviews interfere with a birthday party; or donors need to be personally contacted before a hard deadline; or phone banks or grassroots canvassing need to be manned; and impromptu meetings are called, and on and on. There will be countless pop-ups of unforeseen circumstances that will take precedence over everything else, or you take the risk of losing everything in an uncertain political battle by not doing just "a little more."

One of the biggest problems with saying the family is your highest priority is that during a political war you'll inevitably end up disappointing them and giving the impression you're either insincere or lying to them (**Ecclesiastes 5:4-5**). No matter what you do, that impression will take a lot of time to change after the political winds calm down (e.g., fulfilling **Matthew 3:8**). Even worse for them, if you're elected to office, you can expect the demands on you to continue to be very high.

A more prudent approach would be to talk with your family (or dependents, or "significant other") and explain the situation in an honest (not Pollyannaish) way. For a season, your focus and attention will be elsewhere. It doesn't mean your family isn't more important to you than politics (biblically, family is your priority, see **Exodus 20:12; 2 Corinthians 12:14; Ephesians 6:4a; Colossians 3:21; 1 Timothy 3:4-5; 5:8**), but it does mean the attention given to your family will be restricted as you handle other serious matters for a season.

Everyone, including families, understands emergencies (**Luke 10:29-37**). What they won't accept is double mindedness or inconsistency between what's said and what's done. This is particularly true when back-to-back cycles of *du jour* political issues never end, and preparation for the next election cycle is always just round the corner.

One final thought: you (with your family) need to figure out whether this is the right season of your life to make such a commitment. There's a time and a season for everything (**Ecclesiastes 3:1-8**), and you can't gain back lost time. So, waiting until your family is a lot older, and you're more mature, may be the best decision of all.

PRINCIPLE #15
HOW ARE YOU WITH TEMPTATIONS?

"No temptation has overtaken you that is not common to man.
God is faithful, and he will not let you be tempted beyond your
ability, but with the temptation he will also provide the way of
escape, that you may be able to endure it"
1 Corinthians 10:13

Politics can be energizing, challenging, and exciting. Being around like-minded people that are committed to accomplishing something of import creates a personal closeness that can be unique and intoxicating. And, just as believers are to rejoice with those that rejoice, and weep with those that weep (**Romans 12:15**), so political campaigns can generate the same intense emotions and personal relationships.

Whether you're single or married, these "close encounters" in shared experiences can create affections towards someone else that may be hard to resist. This will be even more tempting when respect begins to turn into adoration or unhealthy desires towards the other person.

Emotional intimacy, just like sexual attraction can develop very innocently, but end up being profoundly destructive traps if allowed to grow when it shouldn't be allowed to do so (**Proverbs 6:32-33**). As flattering as these situations may be, are you mature enough to recognize them and not mentally tease yourself into justifying sinful behavior (**James 1:12-15**)? So, what should you do when compromising situations begin to occur?

First and foremost, remember you're to be above reproach with not even a hint of sexual impurity (**Ephesians 5:3-4**). This is a high standard, but one that's intended for your good and to protect the name of Jesus Christ. Ultimately, you're God's representative in this world (**John 17:18**), and what you do and say will reflect directly on your personal testimony for Christ.

So, are you willing to put "safeguards" in place to help ensure you don't succumb to inappropriate behavior or sexual immorality? Are you willing to not be alone with a co-worker of the opposite sex for any amount of time? Are you willing to not engage in suggestive comments, clever innuendo, inappropriate flirtation, course or off-color joking, or any other behavior that would be sexually suggestive or seem to be inviting inappropriate behavior (**Ephesians 5:3-4; 1 Timothy 5:1b-2**)?

But there's more. Are you flattered when someone of the opposite sex (particularly someone that wields a lot of authority or influence) shows personal interest in you that is beyond just the needs of the campaign? Do you have the wisdom to be able to identify compromising situations as well as the good judgment to prevent yourself from becoming entangled? Are you able to explain what cautions you are taking and how those steps support your commitment to honoring the Lord? Are you mature enough to handle awkward situations that could be easily misunderstood by your co-workers?

And last, but not least: do you have an older, mature believer that can hold you accountable and advise you in any relationships with the potential to develop into more than just a working relationship? Remember, accountability will only be successful if you are transparent and willing to be honest with yourself and others.

The Lord provides safeguards to those He loves. His Word equips you in how you're to behave and treat others. His Spirit guides you in making wise decisions and standing strong in the face of potentially ungodly temptations (**Proverbs 3:5-6**). The Spirit also gives you discernment to identify when situations could lead to ungodly actions (**1 Corinthians 2:12**). And finally, the Lord gives mature advisors to help you navigate life and ministry in a way that pleases the Lord (**Proverbs 13:20**). God provides all these tools as He fulfills His promise to help you make godly, Christ-honoring decisions when you're tempted (**1 Corinthians 10:13**).

PART 4:
POLITICS AND A
KINGDOM-MINDED CHURCH

"Politics" is a dirty word in many churches, but why is that? God has given churches everything they need to equip believers to live a life that honors the Lord in every legitimate pursuit. And, serving the public good through governmental and political involvement is an honorable pursuit if done for the Lord. Where better to understand the spiritual significance of the issues of the day that impact our nation, or to be taught by gifted teachers that know how to apply God's Word with wisdom, or to be held accountable to live a godly life in a difficult environment? When the church overlooks this opportunity for significant impact, it is doing so at its own peril.

PRINCIPLE #16
CHURCHES CAN LEGALLY ENGAGE IN THE POLITICAL REALM

"And let us not grow weary of doing good, for in due season we will reap, if we do not give up. So then, as we have opportunity, let us do good to everyone, and especially to those who are of the household of faith"
Galatians 6:9-10

Your interest in politics probably didn't come from hearing sermons on how important it is to be a godly citizen and actively engage the political and governmental realms. In fact, more than likely your interest is a result of seeing what's happening all around you, or a friend convinced you of the need to "do something, anything."

Once you realized the need, you probably also noticed a lack of interest in politics by your church. If that's the case, you're not alone. The vast majority of church leadership in our nation has concluded that church involvement in politics is verboten. They believe it's either illegal, violates a 501(c)3 status, is not biblical, is too controversial or divisive, is not important, or maybe it's some combination of these factors.

The cold, hard reality is that it's not illegal (or unbiblical) for churches to address any or all political issues. They are free to lobby (encourage) our elected leaders to make godly decisions, call leaders to task for making ungodly decisions, encourage members to register to vote, conduct bipartisan candidate forums, handout non-partisan voter guides, and do many other activities as long as there isn't any formal candidate endorsement and the amount of "political activity" isn't significant compared to the total ministry of the church. Clearly, the church should not become a Political Action Committee (PAC); it's to be a church first and foremost!

The question that needs to be asked is why a public issue becomes the biblical equivalent of "unclean" when someone arbitrarily says it's political? In effect, "politics" has become the one area of church ministry that must be ignored at all costs. Not only is this not biblical (**2 Timothy 3:16-17**), but it defies logic, reason, and ignores the legal protections churches have that are enshrined in our Constitution (i.e. the 1ˢᵗ Amendment).

It's one thing when church leadership consciously ignores speaking to the issues of the day and purposely refuses to equip membership to influence the government. It's quite another for leadership to use supposed legality excuses to justify ignoring our biblical mandate to be: wise counselors to the nation (**Proverbs 11:14; 15:22; 20:18; 24:6**), to expose evil (**Ephesians 5:11**), and to directly influence governments to do the good God has created governments to do (**Romans 13:1-4**).

Why is it important to understand the freedom churches have? So you can wisely help leadership to enter these troubled waters, and to do it in a manner consistent with enduring biblical principles.

Churches are to obey the government, but not at the cost of disobeying God (**Acts 4:19-20; 5:29**), or refusing to preach and teach the entire counsel of God on all matters including elections, laws, justice, and the role of the government. If your church is ignoring this important ministry area, maybe it needs an intervention to wake it up to its high calling to further the kingdom of God in the "political" realm. In fact, maybe you're the one that needs to be the mature, humble one to engineer that intervention. If not you, then who else is going to do it?

Realistically, where else but the church will you turn for godly advice, where else are you going to be held accountable for your decisions, and how else will you be taught what God's Word says about today's issues and the good works that need to be done?

Your involvement in politics is part of the good works that can be done for the good of everyone, just as **Galatians 6:9-10** teaches. And, your church should be helping you do that, biblically.

PRINCIPLE #17

EVERY MORAL ISSUE IS A POLITICAL ISSUE, AND EVERY POLITICAL ISSUE IS A MORAL ISSUE

"If you say, 'Behold, we did not know this,' does not he who weighs the heart perceive it? Does not he who keeps watch over your soul know it, and will he not repay man according to his work?"
Proverbs 24:12

It's sad, but the political divide in our nation is also mirrored in our churches. Not only is there a rift among Christians concerning the applicability of biblical truth to the issues of the day, but there's also a deep divide about whether churches should be engaged in anything that even has the appearance of being political.

Any church denying the inerrancy of Scripture, and not teaching the Bible is sufficient "for all matters of faith and practice" is judging God's truth instead of submitting to it. Those churches have probably already gone far down the path of embracing worldly wisdom and worldviews instead of relying on biblical ones (**Revelation 2:4; 3:1-3,15-18**). As a result, they will almost certainly be counterproductive (if not actually destructive) if they get involved with political matters.

For Bible-believing and preaching/teaching churches, those with a high view of Scripture, there's a divide between those that see the importance of influencing governmental power and those that see no direct church role. Although the latter may be "hands-off" concerning politics, the leadership will likely still confront common moral problems from a biblical perspective. The distinction between the two approaches is often an artificial delineation between what's "moral" and what's considered "political."

There are at least two major problems with drawing a line between political and moral. The first is that the Bible makes no such distinction. In fact, the nature of the **Matthew 5:13-16** salt-and-light imperative is that it applies to every legitimate endeavor in life, whether it is: personal, political, recreational, career, ministry, or whatever. If by "political" church leaders are only thinking in terms of exercising ruthless power, back room deals, cut-throat character assassination, etc., it does a disservice to the entirety of proper governmental functions that by nature should be deliberative, God-honoring, and with a measured degree of compromise for the benefit of the nation's citizens.

The second problem is that every moral issue of any consequence to the believing community is also a political issue. Think about abortion, who educates your child, what constitutes marriage, using lethal force to protect your family, end-of-life medical decisions, gathering for worship during a pandemic, immigration, and on and on. Every one of these is a political "hot potato" that will eventually, negatively, impact churches and individual religious freedoms, both publically and privately, if ignored by the Christian community.

Looking at it from the governmental side, every decision (policy, law, regulation, or action) has a moral basis behind it. The further that basis is from biblical principles, the greater the probability of destructive consequences (**Proverbs 4:27**) resulting from those decisions. To deny there's a moral factor behind all government activities is to deny the influence of human nature itself and the need to wisely restrain it (**Jeremiah 17:9**).

In your political journey, consider carefully where you'll be spiritually equipped the most competently for the inevitable difficulties that politics involves. Where will you be properly held accountable and taught how to navigate controversial situations and what the best policy positions are to figuratively "fight" for? The more restrictive the kingdom perspective of a church, the more isolated the horizon of ministry vision, the less you'll receive the strengthening that **2 Timothy 3:16-17** promises to provide.

PRINCIPLE #18

IF YOU DON'T STAND UP FOR RIGHTEOUSNESS IN THE POLITICAL REALM, WHO WILL?

"The wicked flee when no one pursues,
but the righteous are bold as a lion"
Proverbs 28:1

"For God gave us a spirit not of fear but of power
and love and self-control"
2 Timothy 1:7

Most parents want the best for their children, and try to help them make wise choices in schooling, college, and pursuing a successful career. Professional interests often promoted include becoming a doctor, engineer, lawyer or professor, or even acquiring specialized skills for any number of new technology areas. If you're especially gifted in the arts, you may be encouraged to pursue painting, writing, music, or architecture.

Likewise, the best and brightest in churches may be advised to pursue ministry leadership such as preaching, teaching, youth ministry, music, or even becoming a missionary. Whether by family or church, you'll be encouraged to lead a godly life that honors the Lord, to work hard and with excellence, provide for your family, and be honest and of good character in whatever career you pursue.

Interestingly, the commonality between both family and the church will be a lack of any encouragement for our most promising young men and women to pursue a political career. Why is that?

On the one hand, the world is wide open for you to follow your dreams and enjoy them to the fullest (**Ecclesiastes 5:18-20**). But on the other hand, either by purposeful or inadvertent omission, political achievement (read that as statesmanship) seems to be a non-existent option.

You have Christian liberty to choose a field of interest for either a vocation or avocation. And in fact, many different professions can provide you with the opportunity to make a difference. But consider this: the government has by far had the greatest impact on every single person's life, more so than probably anything else in history – whether that impact was for good, or for evil.

When political involvement (much less running for elective office) isn't even discussed in the home or church, there's a subtle message: that "career" is unworthy of your time, energy, or interest. Is it any wonder that politics has generally come to be seen as unworthy of personal involvement, and that it is corrupt, dirty, destructive, or even evil?

But consider this, what happens when Christian influence is removed from any profession? That profession will rot! What happened in Old Testament Israel when there were no longer godly leaders in the land? They quickly drifted into ungodly pursuits and the nation (and its people) suffered the inevitable consequences (**Deuteronomy 28:1-68**).

Wisdom alone would say the church should work to keep the government within its proper domain so that the church can continue to freely proclaim the gospel and minister to the world. One way to help do that is by consistently encouraging godly involvement by its membership. Consider **Proverbs 29:2,** which says "When the righteous increase, the people rejoice, but when the wicked rule, the people groan."

God has gifted His people for every good work (**2 Timothy 3:16-17**). And, He provides the balance of boldness, wisdom, and self-discipline (**2 Timothy 1:7**) that is sorely lacking in our current super-charged political environment. If you and others walk away, who else will fill the vacuum left behind? Wouldn't it be far more wise and beneficial to follow Isaiah's example and say: "Here am I! Send me" (**Isaiah 6:8**)?

PRINCIPLE #19

CHRISTIANS ARE THE SALT AND LIGHT IN THIS WORLD; GOVERNMENT IS NOT

"You are the salt of the earth, but if salt has lost its taste, how shall its saltiness be restored? It is no longer good for anything except to be thrown out and trampled under people's feet. You are the light of the world. A city set on a hill cannot be hidden. Nor do people light a lamp and put it under a basket, but on a stand, and it gives light to all in the house"
Matthew 5:13-15

God intended the government to be a blessing to its people by properly executing justice, and encouraging the growth of good (**Romans 13:1-4**). It was never intended to replace the good works God's people are commanded to do (**Job 29:15-17; Matthew 7:12; 22:39; 2 Corinthians 1:3-4; Galatians 6:10**).

There are good reasons for this division of responsibility. A secular government that is not grounded in biblical principles will not be able to correctly diagnose the heart issues that cause so much of society's problems (**1 Thessalonians 5:14**); it can only punish bad behaviors (**Romans 13:4**). Without proper diagnosis, government "help" will more than likely make the problems worse instead of better.

Secondly, the government will never point a person to the real remedy for sinful behaviors that originate from a sinful heart (**Luke 6:43-45; Galatians 5:19-21**): that remedy is becoming a new creature in Christ Jesus (**2 Corinthians 5:17**). But what about the inevitable consequences of actions that may or may not be the result of sinful patterns?

When the government creates societal "safety nets" (e.g., welfare programs, entitlement programs, long term unemployment benefits, disaster relief financial grants, industry bailouts, debt forgiveness, and many other social services and security benefits) it creates both dependency and also disincentives to cultivating personal responsibility for oneself and one's family. This isn't true in every case, but exceptions don't justify massive government intervention into millions of lives with the wrong answers to life's problems, particularly if those problems are caused by sin.

The true "safety nets" for a healthy society come from understanding (and accepting) God's biblical design for a nation's people. First, everyone must assume responsibility for their lives (**Psalm 90:17; 128:1-2; Proverbs 12:11,24; 13:4; 14:23; 21:25-26; Galatians 6:4-5**). When circumstances are beyond one's control, the family is the best, next source of help (**1 Timothy 5:8**). This makes sense since the family will have a better idea of the real needs, and will also provide the required accountability. The next ring of help is the church (**Matthew 5:44; 22:39; Galatians 6:10; 1 Timothy 6:18**), allowing it to excel at what it is good at: exemplifying Christ-like mercy and compassion to those that are suffering, whether they are Christians or not (**Matthew 25:31-46**). The church is also gifted with people that can discern true needs and how to properly address them, whether those needs are physical, mental, emotional, or spiritual. The community at large can also provide temporary help, but it can easily suffer from the same shortcomings that government involvement will have.

Government policies that incentivize government to be the first provider of choice for help are contrary to God's design. Realistically, the government should be the last place to turn to. The government should, however, promote conditions helpful in nurturing personal responsibility and also allowing the faith community to minister without getting in their way.

The bottom line is that the government is not God's vehicle to be salt and light; it can never be the true source of salt and light; and it must not co-opt the Christian church's duty to be salt and light to the world (**Matthew 5:13-16**).

Principle #20
Every Legitimate Vocation That Christians Ignore Will Eventually Rot

"I passed by the field of a sluggard, by the vineyard of a man
lacking sense, and behold, it was all overgrown with thorns;
the ground was covered with nettles,
and its stone wall was broken down"
Proverbs 24:30-31

Ever since the fall in the Garden of Eden, the world has been under the curse of God (**Genesis 3:17-19; Romans 8:18-22**). This means that for anything to be fruitful, or even to be maintained, it will take focused effort (work).

Likewise, if something is ignored it will probably decay. What happens when a car doesn't have routine maintenance, or an orchard isn't tended, or a home and yard are not properly kept up, or worn parts aren't replaced on an airplane? Since decay is a universal attribute for material things, doesn't it make sense that the same principle applies to organizations?

Committed Christians, taught and equipped throughout the ages in God's truth, have invested themselves in producing good works that have benefited all of mankind. A short listing of contributions and creative genius includes: educational institutions, hospitals, medicine, the nursing profession, scientific endeavor, the arts, theater, philanthropy, music, literature, equality of men and women, and even politics.

But like everything else that falls within man's "work it and keep it" mandate (**Genesis 2:15**), if godly influence is withdrawn the inevitable result is corruption and decay. As sanctity of life beliefs become less dominant, abortion, infanticide, eugenics, and physician-assisted suicide become more acceptable. As the sanctity of marriage is downplayed, divorce, co-habitation, and perverted forms of marriage receive approval. As universities and colleges originally founded to honor Jesus Christ are no longer shepherded, they become not only secular and leftist but bastions of anti-Christian sentiment.

This phenomenon of godless decay can be seen in every profession and human activity. When godly influence is removed or becomes weak or compromised, rot sets in and anti-Christian sentiment and secular worldviews gain influence and then eventual control.

When the church becomes more inward than outward focused, it loses its evangelistic zeal (**Matthew 28:18-20**) and passion to be salt and light (**Matthew 5:13-16**). It can easily become more of an enjoyer of the blessings of its prior outreach rather than an initiator of them. Instead of equipping believers to be enthusiastic about every good work (**2 Timothy 3:16-17**), it can become focused on internal church good works. By becoming comfortable, the general church can become content with itself and only a commentator on the times instead of a force to engage and change the times for God's glory. Not only is this lukewarm attitude condemned biblically (**Revelation 3:15-19**), but in the arena of politics and the use of governmental power it can become devastating to Christian kingdom work as antagonistic forces end up taking control of the levers of power.

Biblically, the church with its teachers and preachers is the perfect place to equip and send believers out into the world to work for the common good (**Jeremiah 29:7**) and apply righteous standards to every endeavor under the sun. Jesus Himself sent out His disciples to change the world (**Mark 6:7-13; Luke 10:1-12; Acts 1:6-8**); shouldn't this be our pattern, especially while godly people still have an opportunity to influence governments in a godly manner?

Principle #21

The Best Place To Mentor Future Politicians Is Within The Church

"Blessed be the Lord, my rock, who trains my hands for war,
and my fingers for battle"
Psalm 144:1

Politics is more than just a non-contact sport; it quite literally has life and death consequences for individuals and families that are impacted by governmental decisions every day. In short, politics is not a game; it's very serious business.

Churches excel at preparing members to fulfill godly roles in marriage and as parents. Men and women are taught to develop a good work ethic, godly character, honesty, and other moral qualities that will serve them well in their chosen profession. How much more important is it then, to equip men and women (young and old) that want to serve in the morally confusing, hostile, and many times ungodly realm of politics (**Ephesians 6:10-12**)?

As **Psalm 144:1** says, the Lord trains us for war. He does that by gifting His church with people that understand conflict and are willing to guide those willing to fight the good fight in environments hostile to Christian influence. Spiritual warfare is exactly what the term implies: warfare. And the Lord isn't going to lead us into battle without resources, no matter how complicated the political circumstances. Consider Solomon, he was a king gifted by God to understood the difficulty of governing a people of divided interests and loyalties (**1 Kings 3:5-12; Proverbs 1:8-19; 2:1-15**). Is it any different for leaders in government today?

Pastors may not have detailed knowledge of political issues, but they have a wealth of insight into what will please the Lord. They'll also know those within the church that are mature in understanding political environments and have the best insights to mentor those that want to enter these tricky waters.

In fact, many of the spiritual gifts mentioned in **Romans 12:4-8, 1 Corinthians 12:4-7** and other places of Scripture (i.e., helps, administration, discernment, exhortation, giving, hospitality, knowledge, leadership, serving, wisdom, etc.) are abilities that are very useful in public service. For elected leaders especially, objectively knowing one's strengths and weaknesses will help determine who needs to be brought alongside to help provide proper balance in facing decisions. Where else but the church would someone turn to gain this type of wisdom and insight?

How does this type of equipping play out in an environment with so many wolves in sheep's clothing (**Matthew 7:15-20; Romans 16:18; 2 Corinthians 11:14-15**)? It takes committed prayer (**1 Timothy 2:1-2**), wise counsel (**Proverbs 11:14; 15:22; 19:20-21; 24:6; James 1:5**), standing firm (**Ephesians 6:11; 1 Peter 5:8-9**), and recognizing who are enemies and who are friends (**Romans 12:2, Hebrews 5:14**). The church can equip in all these areas.

Political careers are legitimate works of service. Secular seminars, volunteer work, election classes, online instruction all have their place. But for you to understand the strengths and weaknesses of giftedness, to be trained in character development and how to resist temptation, and to have access to wise counsel it's all within the church. That's also where you'll learn how to apply a biblical worldview to the complex issues of our day. It may not be in the detailed specifics you want, but you will have access to the needed spiritual understanding and wisdom to do it right.

Finally, positions of public influence should be sought, but not for personal glory or prideful reasons. They should only be sought to bring glory to God. And always remember, political temptations and challenges aren't unique to life, but they'll have their unique twists and turns that God has gifted others to help you successfully understand and cope with.

50

PART 5:
THE ENIGMA OF GOVERNMENT

I n the vernacular of the day, the church has a "love-hate" relationship
with government. On the one hand, government is a blessing to us all
since it was brought into existence for our good. On the other hand, it can
become a ruthless enemy of the gospel and something to be resisted. So
how are "church and state" supposed to relate to each other? Are there any
overlapping roles between the two, or is each completely separate from the
other? The answers to these types of questions rely on an understanding
of the nature of mankind, and the limitations of government, no matter
what form government takes.

PRINCIPLE #22
THERE ARE NO TRUE CHRISTIAN NATIONS, ONLY CHRISTIANIZED ONES

"But you are a chosen race, a royal priesthood,
a holy nation, a people for his own possession,
that you may proclaim the excellencies of him who called
you out of darkness into his marvelous light"
1 Peter 2:9

As tempting as it may be to say the United States is a "Christian nation," there's no clear biblical mandate for such a thing to exist before the Lord returns (**Revelation 20:1-6**).

There have been nations, the United States being the most prominent, powerful, and influential, that were Christianized. That is to say, Christianity was historically the dominant shared culture, the source of a common societal moral foundation, and unquestionably influential in the creation of a system of justice and the definition and allocation of governmental responsibilities.

Even though God's truths were clearly instrumental in our nation's development, we didn't make Christianity the nation's official religion, or the Bible the supreme law of the land with the Constitution and all other laws conforming to it.

Colloquially the United States is commonly referred to as being a Christian nation (as opposed to being a Muslim or Buddhist nation) because it contains so many Christians. However, as a nation the United States has been both a blessing to the world (e.g. through just laws, military protection, civil and human rights, medical advances, benevolence, missionaries, technology, etc.) as well as a moral polluter of the world (e.g. through pornography, human trafficking, special LGBT rights, normalization of sexual impurity, promotion of abortion, etc.) as it becomes more secularized. These latter influences are clearly inconsistent with being Christian.

Why distinguish between a "historically Christianized nation" and officially being a "Christian nation?" It's important because politically our nation has become far more multi-cultural, multi-racial, and multi-religious. It also has many atheists, agnostics, pure secularists, and a wide spectrum of Christian adherents ranging from very progressive (if not outright socialists) to the very theologically and politically conservative. Given that environment, if you say the United States a "Christian nation," or you want to "take the country back for Jesus," or you want to "reclaim the nation for Christ;" you are sending a powerful message to others that you want some form of a Christian theocracy with Old Testament laws becoming the law of the land. That may not be your goal, but that's what is heard; and that's what will alienate many that otherwise may have supported your moral causes.

Among Christians, understanding this distinction without being dogmatic helps prevent unnecessary time and energy from being wasted in arguing about which view is most accurate. Historical statements by our nation's founders, U.S. Supreme Court pronouncements, secular claims against anything Christian, and even selected biblical references (**Psalm 24:1; Zechariah 14:9**) can all provide fodder to argue the case for either side. But the bottom line is whether it's worth fighting over. That battle may only cause unnecessary divisiveness among Christians and put focus on inconsequential matters instead of more important concerns, much to the delight of the political left.

Regardless of where you stand, the one fact we can be sure of biblically is that the Body of Christ, universally, is a holy nation unto itself (**1 Peter 2:9**) with Jesus Christ as its King of kings and Lord of lords (**Deuteronomy 10:17; Psalm 136:3; 1 Timothy 6:15; Revelation 17:14, 19:16**).

The Lord's nation has no borders, it will not perish, and it will be supernaturally protected by Him against all threats whether they are foreign or domestic (**Matthew 16:18**)!

PRINCIPLE #23
SCRIPTURE DOESN'T MANDATE ANY SPECIFIC FORM OF GOVERNMENT

"Let every person be subject to the governing authorities.
For there is no authority except from God, and those
that exist have been instituted by God"
Romans 13:1

Scripture gives no formula for how a government should be structured. In fact, references to governmental authority in the New Testament (**Romans 13:1-2; 1 Timothy 2:1-2; 1 Peter 2:13-14**) imply that any authority structure is to be obeyed when it fulfills its duty to implement justice and promote good. Old Testament examples of governance include a form of dictatorship with Moses under the authority of the Lord (**Exodus**), a military dictatorship (**Joshua**), regional judges (**Judges 2:11,16**), monarchies (**1 Samuel 8:4-5**), and a theocracy (**1 Samuel 8:7**). Whatever the form a government may take, Scripture says if it honors the Lord, it will be blessed (**Proverbs 14:34**).

The government of the United States is unique in history with both its structural form and restrictions at the federal (national) level to only a limited set of enumerated powers. Its genius includes recognition of a balance of authority and power that are a reflection of the Lord's very nature, a nature comprised of Lawgiver (Congress), Judge (Supreme Court), and King (President) (**Isaiah 33:22**).

Unfortunately, for over a generation the political winds in the United States have been rapidly shifting to embrace a socialist type of government that is intrinsically godless (secular only) and focused on gaining absolute power over everyone and everything.

If you are able to look objectively at the history of governments over the last hundred years, ask yourself which ones have resulted in the mass extermination of life, political imprisonment of its citizens, widespread misery, and the elimination of personal freedoms and individual entrepreneurship? The answer is obvious: regimes based on secular humanist worldviews that reject any concept of God, devalue human life, and elevate the government as the ultimate authority above everything else. These constructs include Marxism, fascism, communism, and Nazis, with socialism being a milder precursor to gain acceptance by citizens of ever-increasing levels of tyranny.

For almost two hundred and fifty years, however, there's one specific nation that prospered, grew wealthy and powerful, implemented a flawed but improvable justice system, protected individual freedoms, and encouraged initiative and opportunity. That nation is the United States. Though troubled today with major sinful tendencies, the nation's founding was clearly guided by biblical principles. These included an understanding of the sinful nature of mankind, the resulting need to prevent the government from being able to accumulate unlimited power, and a prevailing desire to honor the Lord.

It's no surprise that our national blessings are still dependent on seeking God's will to inform governance and a clear acknowledgment of a higher authority to which our nation is accountable (**Job 12:23**). Not only is this biblical (**Proverbs 14:34**), but it is explicitly stated in our nation's Declaration of Independence.

With that understanding, any exercise of political power (or governmental structure) must be evaluated in terms of whether it brings our nation closer to God or further away from Him. The consequences of going down the wrong path (i.e., first towards socialism and then to even more godless tyrannies) are catastrophic (**Deuteronomy 28:1-67**), and must be resisted wherever possible for the common good of individuals, families, our nation, and particularly for our religious liberties.

PRINCIPLE #24

BECAUSE GOVERNMENT MAGNIFIES MAN'S NATURE, IT MUST BE RESTRAINED

"So Pilate said to him, 'You will not speak to me? Do you not know that I have authority to release you and authority to crucify you?' Jesus answered him, 'You would have no authority over me at all unless it had been given you from above.'"
John 19:10-11a

Contrary to what so many want to believe, the unredeemed nature of man is desperately wicked (**Jeremiah 17:9**), and has no desire to seek out and obey the true God (**Romans 3:10-18**) before whom they will give an account of their lives (**Ecclesiastes 12:13-14; Romans 2:1-6**).

World history demonstrates conclusively that when power is placed in the hands of those that are ruthless, wickedness is emboldened and the people will suffer (**Proverbs 29:2b**). For our day it doesn't matter whether that power was stolen (i.e., through fraudulent elections or a military coup), purposely handed to them through fair elections, or "fell" into their possession (i.e., through line of succession or appointment), the consequences of sinful natures wielding any power over others is to be feared.

As more power is aggregated (i.e., with the President, a governor, or a mayor), the greater the opportunity for power to metastasize at the expense of others. Wicked hearts may accomplish some good through sheer force, but in the end those small gains can never justify ignoring the government's proper, limited role of executing justice and promoting the common good (**Romans 13:1-4; 1 Peter 2:13-14**). Pure democracies are also subject to abuse if the general moral fabric of society becomes corrupt.

Because of man's basic nature, true, broad-based democracies will never work, neither will socialism nor communism. These idealized (utopian) constructs assume mankind is not only fundamentally good (i.e., without need for any redemptive change), but that they will always act in the best interests of others no matter what the personal cost.

The founders of our nation understood the nature of mankind and sought to implement a system of governance that at its most powerful level (national) would be restrained to only having "enumerated" powers and nothing else. Even Pilate did not have unlimited power; what authority he did have was given by God to fulfill His eternal purposes relative to Christ's redemptive mission (**John 19:10-11a**).

Legally restraining the extent of power is specifically intended to prevent the growth of unrestrained power, which the founders knew would eventually (and quickly) become corrupt. Conversely, more latitude was allowed to exist for direct governance by the people at the local level, where ruthless leaders could be removed from power through elections or legal action. Our system of governance "worked" when first formed because of many prior years of dominant Christian influence at the community level that valued justice and moral standards based on a biblical worldview.

Unfortunately, even the genius of the United States Constitution cannot overcome widespread societal corruption and destructive self-interest if people are not generationally schooled in biblical values (**Proverbs 22:6**) and see the benefits in living by them. When institutions of governance, political leaders, and society in general throw off self-restraint, then widespread anarchy and unrest, followed by strong-armed oppression will naturally follow.

Government doesn't give up power easily; it must be forced to do so. As Christians, the means we have available to continually "reform" governance include: direct political engagement, always seeking ways to limit governmental overreach, and educating as many as possible to accept the benefits of God's common grace through wise application of biblical values. Fail at this, and we will eventually go the way of all prior empires.

GOVERNMENT IS A MORALLY NEUTRAL, VERY BLUNT TOOL

"If the iron is blunt, and one does not sharpen the edge,
he must use more strength, but wisdom helps one to succeed"
Ecclesiastes 10:10

I t almost goes without saying that the larger an organization, the more inefficient, relatively ineffective, and self-serving it can become. It's not surprising therefore, that government by its nature is not an entity that should be turned to for a quick, cost-effective response to any crisis, much less trying to address human problems of the heart or soul. The rare exception to this rule is the military, which is very effective at destroying an enemy. But it took, and continues to take, trillions of dollars to build and keep that capability.

That being said, the government is never described as intrinsically evil in Scripture, it does not have a soul or any natural attribute that will be judged (i.e., punished or rewarded) by God. In essence, it is nothing more or less than a massive, powerful, blunt tool that can be used for evil or for good. When it's restrained to the roles it was created by God to carry out, the government is a blessing as it restrains evil and supports good (**Romans 13:1-4; 1 Timothy 2:1-2; 1 Peter 2:13-14**). On the other hand, when its intrinsic power (**Romans 13:4**) is put into the hands of evil people, it can be unbelievably destructive and wicked.

Why is this important to understand? It's important because the government in its simplest form is an enormous, powerful expression of the values of its citizens. When society becomes corrupt, is lacking in restraint, is self-indulgent, is unrestrained sexually, and becomes ungrateful and hateful it will despise anything that reflects God's holy nature. This includes His people, His Word, and especially the gospel of Jesus Christ.

Another way to say it is this: when the hopelessness of godless secular worldviews (e.g. socialism, communism, humanism, atheism, etc.) (**Colossians 2:8**) are embraced instead of God's revealed pattern and principles for success and blessings, then irrational hatred inevitably turns against what's good and wholesome. Not only that, but broken ideologies will always turn to their weapon of choice – coercive governmental power – to force conformance to their destructive ideas when they can't convince enough people to go along with them willingly.

When the government is used for purposes for which it was not intended, it takes a lot of legal, economic, and brute physical force, coupled with compliant social and media power, to make people conform to its bidding (**Ecclesiastes 10:10**). With the government being the wrong tool implementing wrong ideas about reality, the results are guaranteed to be catastrophic.

This situation is particularly true when wicked politicians affirm or even promote evil behaviors as if they were good, and then treating what is clearly, traditionally and biblically known to be good as if it were evil (**Isaiah 5:20-21**). This is the downward moral path that ultimately results in the utter collapse of a nation into chaos, followed by tyranny.

On the other hand, when the tool of government is used wisely to focus on fulfilling its God-ordained purposes people will be blessed and a society will thrive (**Proverbs 29:2**).

Bottom line: the government is no more and no less, a cumbersome, blunt tool that needs to be used both wisely and narrowly in application. Otherwise, it will cause far more damage than any blessings that may happen to occur.

PRINCIPLE #26

GOVERNMENT IS NOT TO BE TREATED LIKE IT'S A CHURCH

*"Therefore render to Caesar the things that are Caesar's,
and to God the things that are God's"*
Matthew 22:21

This may sound like an obvious truth, but the government is not an extension of the church. It is not a ministry that the church individually, in aggregate, or denominationally can direct and conform to its bidding. In fact, government and the church occupy two distinctively different, but mutually supportive realms of authority (**Matthew 22:21**).

Governments have existed from the earliest of times, ever since cities began forming (**Genesis 4:17**). They are part of God's plan to maintain order in a fallen world that is prone to creating anarchy and chaos (**Romans 13:4; 1 Timothy 2:1-2**).

The true church is comprised of everyone called out of the world and given citizenship in God's kingdom (**Philippians 3:20**). Even though believers are members of a spiritual nation (**1 Peter 3:9**), they have a dual citizenship responsibility that obligates them to submit to earthly governments (**Romans 13:1-2**). However, this submission to the government is not absolute, it is conditioned on government not assuming authority it does not have (**Acts 5:29**).

Both the governmental and church realms are accountable to God (**Daniel 2:21; Ephesians 5:24a**). But the church is entrusted with temporal spiritual matters that have eternal implications (**Ephesians 3:10-12**), while governments have authority throughout the earth over temporal matters necessary for the exercise of justice and the creation of an environment supportive of the common good (**Romans 13:1-4**).

But there are even more distinctive differences between the two. First, the church is not to be "yoked" to the government no matter how many Christians may be serving in public office and exercising governmental authority (**2 Corinthians 6:14-16**). Being bound together would eventually compromise the church's unique ability to bring glory to God by being both salt and light, extending loving mercy to the oppressed, and by evangelizing (**Matthew 5:13-16; 22:39; 28:18-20**).

Biblically, the church doesn't appoint government leaders or remove them from government service through church discipline. Also, the church is not to wage war, establish national policy, enforce civil laws, or levy taxes. It does, however, pray for those in government leadership (**1 Timothy 2:1-2**), speak out on moral issues (**Ephesians 5:11**), provide advice and counsel to leadership (**Proverbs 29:18**), equip leaders to serve in public office, and equip members to vote with biblical principles.

Government on the other hand, is not to define what Christianity is, what our beliefs are, or how the church is to be governed. In addition, it is not to appoint church leaders, restrict public expressions or practice of faith, rule on spiritual matters or interfere with the exercise of church discipline (**Matthew 18:15-17**). Because the power to tax is the power to destroy, government is also not to tax churches (**Genesis 47:13-26**). Since a government left to its own devices will eventually become abusive, it needs to allow itself to be wisely shepherded by Christian citizens (**Proverbs 25:15**) that are biblically trained by the church to do so (**2 Timothy 3:16-17**).

The bottom line: government is not some benign, benevolent organization that exists solely for the benefit of the church. It is not a trusted friend or spiritual confidant. Government does, however, protect the church by punishing evildoers in society and providing for the common good through common grace means.

PRINCIPLE #27

THE CONSTITUTION'S 1ST AMENDMENT PROTECTS FREEDOM OF RELIGIOUS CONSCIENCE IN ALL THINGS

"We must obey God rather than men"
Acts 5:29

Our nation came into being to escape religious persecution. It's not surprising, therefore, that religious liberty is guaranteed in our nation's governing document, the Constitution. The 1st Amendment says: "Congress shall make no law respecting an establishment of religion, or prohibiting the free exercise thereof."

This doesn't say you only have the freedom to worship inside chapel walls. It says you're free to exercise your religious freedom anywhere. That means in your chosen profession, in your family, in your community, in your business, as well as in your church and even in elective office. It also means the government has no authority to restrict this freedom. But, like other guaranteed freedoms there are exceptions if that free exercise presents a clear and dangerous threat to life or health.

Religious conscience is a very big deal. Just as the Apostles refused to bend to the ungodly restrictions the religious leaders of their day tried to impose on them (**Acts 4:1-20; 5:17-29**), so this Amendment ensures you don't have to bend to ungodly or misguided restrictions by the government.

Does this constitutional protection mean the government won't try to restrict our religious liberties? Unfortunately, the natural bent of government is to accumulate as much power as possible. And, as government leadership becomes more secularized the laws and policies they implement become less understanding or "tolerant" of Christian beliefs, conscience, decisions and influence.

Without consistent, firm, and wide-ranging Christian influence on the government, laws such as those addressing hate crimes, same-sex marriages, hiring practices, mandating medical insurance for abortion or sex-change operations, help concerning unwanted same-sex attraction, and even taxes will be inappropriately applied to churches as well as businesses and organizations run by Christians. In fact, the well known but purposely deceptive term "separation of church and state" has morphed from protecting religious influence everywhere, into specifically rejecting Christian influence in anything relating to the government or whatever the government touches.

How can these attacks on Christian influence and conscience be happening? To apply a common phrase to our shrinking religious freedoms: you "either use 'em or lose 'em."

The bottom line is that you cannot be just a passive observer of these major attacks on issues of Christian conscience. A completely secular government will fully embrace a worldview that rejects any higher spiritual reality or accountability and will, over time, become openly anti-religious (read that as anti-Christian) by any direct or indirect means at its disposal.

Without Christians seeking and occupying positions of influence in the government to prevent unjust laws to begin with, the only pragmatic option for protection is a justice system with uncertain outcomes. Sadly, without godly influence in the public realm and within the halls of justice, man's ungodly nature (**Jeremiah 17:9, John 8:42-44**) will eventually prevail, or at least make Christianity as difficult as possible to live out.

Not just incidentally, the rest of the 1st Amendment enshrines other liberties that both relate to and protect the freedom of religion: "...freedom of speech, or of the press; or the right of the people peaceably to assemble, and to petition the Government for a redress of grievances." These freedoms must be affirmed and protected as well, or our precious religious freedoms will suffer immeasurably and possibly irretrievably.

PRINCIPLE #28

IF ALLOWED TO DO SO, GOVERNMENT WILL CO-OPT OUR SALT AND LIGHT MANDATE FOR POLITICAL PURPOSES

"When the wicked rise, people hide themselves,
but when they perish, the righteous increase"
Proverbs 28:28

Unrestrained power is a fearful thing to experience. Just ask anyone that has lived under totalitarian regimes. Both the brilliance and blessing of our nation are that its federal powers are enumerated and limited, while our basic freedoms are protected by law at both the national and local levels.

Because we have legally protected rights, it has taken many decades for the United States to become more totalitarian in its use of governmental power. What has aided this abusive growth has been the dramatic removal of direct, biblical Christian influence in governance, and concurrent growth of political self-interest driven by purely secular reasoning (**Colossians 2:8**).

Not surprisingly, significant growth of governmental control and overreach happened when the government adopted Christianity's compassion mandate for its own purposes. By becoming the "go-to" source of societal safety nets to shield people from the consequences of destructive behaviors, "acts of God," and catastrophic events beyond a person's control (**Ecclesiastes 9:11**), the government has become the equivalent of a values-free, benevolent parent. The result: an exploding dependence on unconditional handouts from a politicized bureaucracy for the basics of life. This development co-opts proven church-based interventions and mercy ministries that can diagnose and meet actual human needs with discernment, balance, and accountability (**1 Thessalonians 5:14; 2 Thessalonians 3:10-12**).

Since non-biblical government remedies can't account for the heart-centered source of mankind's problems (**Jeremiah 17:9**), secular "solutions of choice" can only make matters worse. This destructive cycle incentivizes more and more people to become dependent, while bigger government is seen as the only way to "solve" the very problems it helped create.

But the government hasn't just co-opted our biblical mercy responsibilities; it also assumed our stewardship duties (**Genesis 1:28-30; 2:15,20; 9:1-7**) for the environment and all living creatures. With the lack of any widespread, biblically-based creation-care understanding of our need to balance and not abuse the world around us, the government has enthusiastically taken that leadership role and left biblical wisdom and purpose completely out of any solution considerations.

In doing this, the government becomes the ultimate arbiter in how to protect every living thing in the world, no matter what the consequences are to people made in God's image (**Genesis 1:26-27**). Government also decides how much control should be applied to every human activity that can conceivably be linked to influencing the climate or the animal kingdom, no matter how infinitesimally small the effect may be (**Proverbs 1:7; 14:15-16; 15:2; 18:2**).

The above "god-like" actions serve only to consolidate power in the hands of a few and have nothing to do with bringing glory to God. In essence, people, animals, and the climate have become things to control in order to feed the ego of those in charge (**Proverbs 26:12**), to the detriment of the human condition.

There are many people in desperate need that you and other Christians are to minister to, and there's a proper balance between using and conserving the created order around us. But the government shouldn't compete with God's ordained way of addressing sinful behaviors and the particular circumstances of the creation that He intends to use to bring attention and glory to Himself (**Romans 8:28; 1 Corinthians 10:31; Ephesians 2:10**).

PRINCIPLE #29

A SECULAR GOVERNMENT WILL NEVER POINT A PERSON TO CHRIST

"The natural person does not accept the things of the Spirit of God, for they are folly to them, and he is not able to understand them because they are spiritually discerned"
1 Corinthians 2:14

According to God's Word, governments have two primary duties: to execute justice and to promote the common good (**Romans 13:1-4; 1 Timothy 2:1-2; 1 Peter 2:13-14**). These duties are independent of the actual form a government may take (i.e., monarchy, oligarchy, democracy, constitutional republic, etc.).

Throughout history, all forms of government have tacitly or explicitly acknowledged the existence of a divine nature of some kind, distinct from our earthly nature. Recent history, however, has seen the creation of purely secular-humanistic (atheistic) governments that deny the existence of any higher authority. This is explicitly true for communist countries and implicitly true in socialist countries. For purely secular governments, Christian allegiance to the Lord above the state is considered a threat since complete obedience to statist power cannot be assured otherwise.

It's not surprising, therefore, as secular-humanist worldviews become more dominant in our nation's government, that hostility towards our beliefs and values will also become more prevalent. This hostility is not just a matter of indifference; it can eventually become an active purging of values that emanate from a distinctly biblical worldview grounded in the gospel. Consider what happens with many politicians that claim a "personal faith tradition" that allegedly aligns with Christianity. Their decisions concerning issues like the sanctity of life, traditional marriage, the nuclear family, equality of justice, and freedom of religion or self-defense will often expose an opposite conviction (**2 Timothy 3:1-5**).

Because secular governments cannot correctly diagnose the causes of problems intrinsic to a fallen human nature (**Romans 3:10-18**), they will instinctively apply wrong solutions with predictably destructive results. This will be true wherever the government turns its misguided attention: entitlement programs, forced wealth redistribution, controlling the economy, micro-managing the environment, rationing of health care, and even arrogantly trying to control the climate.

The one solution that secular governments will not tolerate is the only one that provides any hope for the health of a person's soul and their ability to make wise life decisions – the gospel of Jesus Christ (**Matthew 6:25-34; 11:25-30**). Secular governments are incapable of giving any credence to spiritual (biblical) solutions because these can only be earnestly understood through the working of the Holy Spirit (**1 Corinthians 2:14**). Blindness like this becomes even more apparent as politicians with humanistic worldviews refuse to allow objective reality (facts) to influence their decisions. This rejection of reason can only reflect one, evil source (**John 8:44**). This assessment may seem harsh, but political battle spiritual warfare and eternal matters at stake.

The truth is, the more our nation slides toward implementing a thoroughly secular-atheistic government, the more intolerance towards any Christian or biblical influence will become the written or unwritten law of the land. When this happens, history shows that public shaming, censorship, discrimination, and eventually criminalization of Christian beliefs and its adherents will follow.

The bottom line: the political frenzy to make the United States into a socialist nation can only be successful if you and other Christians refuse to push back and take the initiative to be open about biblical values and objective truth. As Christians we are not neutral observers, we are all called to resist evil (**1 Peter 5:8-9**), publically expose it (**Ephesians 5:11**), and entrust the eventual results into God's hands (**1 Corinthians 3:6-9**).

Part 6:
Casting a Vote

C asting a vote in any election is a serious matter. In a very tangible way our votes are an expression of our values and an indication of what is important to us. Although our system of voting doesn't require us to do any research into the candidates and issues that appear on the ballot, we each know how much time and effort (if any) we've invested in these important and consequential decisions. But even more importantly, although we know our vote is a secret to those around us, we need to remember that nothing we do is hidden from the Lord.

Principle #30

The Votes Of Both An Ignorant Christian And A Secular Person Are Dangerous

"Do not be conformed to this world, but be transformed by the renewal of your mind, that by testing you may discern what is the will of God, what is good and acceptable and perfect"
Romans 12:2

" **I** f only every Christian voted we could turn this country around." Just because I've heard that phrase countless times, doesn't mean that it is true!

We don't expect the world to see things through the lens (worldview) that God has given us in His Word. In fact, unbelievers are incapable of correctly understanding or sincerely applying spiritual truths to their personal lives and decisions (**1 Corinthians 2:14-16**). But what about the person that self-identifies as a Christian? They may be sweet and compassionate, and even use common biblical words and lingo. But are they immersed enough in God's Word to be discerning towards the ungodly and deceptive messages of the culture we live in? For that matter, do they sufficiently understand God's truths to effectively apply them to the difficult, defining issues of our day?

Part of the answer to that last question is that less than 6% of all Americans have a biblical worldview that informs their life and decisions. What about the other 94%, what about entire liberal "Christian" denominations that don't accept the inerrancy of God's Word or the absolute authority of the Bible? What about those choosing to "self-worship" at home by channel surfing on TV or the internet on Sunday mornings (or late at night) and only pick messages out of curiosity rather than a deep desire to have their sins confronted and their lives committed to follow Christ?

Truth be told, there's a reason why the world sometimes has a hard time believing Christians are any different than them. If a church is little more than a social gathering to you, if the Lordship of Christ is little more than a slogan, and if your heroes and role models tend to be athletes or celebrities, then the pagan world has successfully evangelized you more than you've evangelized them (**Romans 12:2**).

Without a desire to know God's Word and become a light to a darkened and heavily politicized world (**1 Peter 2:12**), you will easily become captive to the smooth talk of deceived hearts (**Psalm 55:21; Romans 16:18**) that fill so much of the social discourse you're exposed to. Without testing these messages against God's Word, you can easily become captive to those that hold to destructive beliefs and also think they know better than God (**Colossians 2:8**).

If you, as a self-identified Christian, identify more with the world than with the kingdom of God, then your politics (and how you vote) will reflect that double-mindedness (**James 1:5-8**). The answer to that problem is not to whip up yourself and every self-identifying Christian into a political lather, but to be convinced that every vote (and the political viewpoint it represents) are decisions for which you'll answer to an almighty God (**Matthew 12:36**).

The bottom line: if you're an ignorant, compromised Christian it's probably better that you don't vote at all, rather than naively "cast your lot" and further the schemes of those that hate Christ and biblical values.

What would be even better, however, is to become informed about the issues and candidates of today, and evaluate them from a biblical perspective. Also, to seek counsel from mature believers that base their decisions on a biblical worldview (**Proverbs 19:20-21**) and learn from them so that your voting decisions honor the Lord and not the world.

PRINCIPLE #31
ALWAYS VOTE FROM A BIBLICAL PERSPECTIVE

"So, whether you eat or drink, or whatever you do,
do all to the glory of God"
1 Corinthians 10:31

I n your lifetime there are a variety of votes you may be privileged to cast. In elections you're voting for candidates for different offices, on whether to adopt statewide propositions or initiatives, and at the local level for approval or disapproval of city or county Measures. If you're in elective office you'll be voting on many proposed laws, policies, ordinances, or even appointments. If you're in a staff position to someone serving in an elective office, you'll be making recommendations on what to support (or not support) and why.

Casting a vote is making a "Yes" or "No" decision that becomes a matter of record. Just like the words we speak, it's not something to take lightly (**Matthew 12:36**). After all, you know you'll eventually have to give an account for everything you've done (**Ecclesiastes 12:13-14; Romans 14:12; 2 Corinthians 5:10**), and God hasn't left you to figure things out on your own. He has given you His extensive Word to guide your life and your decisions (**Psalm 119:105; Matthew 4:4; 2 Timothy 3:16-17**). Knowing all this, you need to continually work at developing a keen and robust biblical worldview that informs everything you do, including all of your votes and recommendations.

Will this be easy? No, it'll take a lot of work. But the more you begin to instinctively think first about what the Bible says, the easier it'll become to have confidence in the decisions that you'll have to make.

When considering the application of a biblical perspective, it's helpful to always have several questions in the back of your mind. The first is: does God's Word directly address this decision, or does it have general principles that should be considered? The second is: will this particular decision honor the Lord and be pleasing to Him (**1 Corinthians 10:31; Ephesians 5:8-10; Colossians 1:9-10**)?

The incredible political polarization in our nation makes many policy and candidate decisions easy. But there will always be some judgments to make that will be complicated because of conflicting interests or loyalties, a variety of competing principles, a lack of perfect and robust information, and even uncertainty concerning future implications.

Not surprisingly, many decisions will require the application of wisdom (**James 1:5**). What this means is that even though contemporary issues may have unique, specific circumstances attached to them, you can be assured there will be eternal, underlying biblical values and moral imperatives that will still apply (**Ecclesiastes 1:1-11; Matthew 24:35**).

Another factor, however, is that your personal convictions may differ from those of someone else (**Romans 14:1-9**). When that happens, you need to ask yourself whether you have the freedom to vote, or provide counsel, that may differ from that of other committed believers. The short answer is that as long as God's Word is not violated (**Acts 5:29**), and your conscience before the Lord is clear (**Acts 24:16**), you have a lot of freedom to apply the principles you've found to be the most appropriate for the given action (**2 Timothy 2:15**). This doesn't necessarily disparage the convictions (or preferences) of others, but it does ensure your decision will be based on a solid foundation and not just personal whimsy.

Finally, the higher the uncertainty on what decision to make, the more important it will be to seek counsel from others with more experience (**Proverbs 19:20-21**). Doing so will keep you accountable, broaden your ability to understand and apply God's Word, and ensure you're not overlooking something important.

PRINCIPLE #32
LONG LISTS OF NON-NEGOTIABLES ARE AN EXCUSE TO DO NOTHING

"Be not overly righteous, and do not make yourself too wise.
Why should you destroy yourself?
Ecclesiastes 7:16

I t's tempting to keep a list of policy positions that you'll not compromise on, and that a candidate must agree with before you'd ever consider voting for them. For biblical Christians the list generally includes sanctity of life, only supporting traditional marriage, family values, religious freedom, and support for Israel. Variations to this listing may include gun ownership, limited government, fiscal responsibility, school vouchers, a strong defense, or any other major issue that is near and dear to you.

We know there's no perfect candidate, but some will be clearly better than others. The question you have to answer is whether your "list" is an absolute qualifying/disqualifying one, or provides factors that are useful in determining the candidate closest to what you want.

Too often, non-negotiable tests for political orthodoxy only serve to reject candidates that may have some solid positions but are weak in one or two areas. The reality is that there will rarely be a candidate that will meet all your requirements. As your "must have" list grows longer, it can almost guarantee that no one will be qualified in your eyes for your vote.

This has a dual effect, neither of which is useful. On the one hand, you make yourself out as the noble, righteous one with a high standard that knows better than anyone else what's needed. Not only that, but being a "non-compromiser" is a subtle message to everyone else that they're wrong and you're the only one right (**Proverbs 14:12; 26:12; Isaiah 5:21**). On the other hand, you're effectively removing yourself from the election process and not helping to prevent some truly horrible candidate from being elected to office.

On one level this situation may be satisfying to you (**Proverbs 21:2**) and appease your conscience, but the reality is that you've made yourself irrelevant to the political, elective process. Should there actually be a candidate that passes muster with your lengthy, political, orthodoxy test, I can almost guarantee that that candidate is virtually unknown to the broader voting community and is going to be unelectable.

A short list of non-negotiables is helpful to differentiate between candidates to find the most qualified (**Exodus 18:21**). But it can be counterproductive if its real effect is to only determine the degree to which all candidates are disqualified.

Wisdom would indicate that when faced with only poor choices, the one closest to your stance on key issues (and that has some possibility of being elected) is the one to support. Where your input can be the most helpful to the broader community of believers is when you help identify those candidates that would be the most harmful to your values. Taking this approach will go a long way to helping ensure those that are unworthy do not obtain elective office.

PRINCIPLE #33
SUPPORT A CANDIDATE CLOSEST TO YOUR VALUES AND THE MOST ELECTABLE

"Better is a neighbor who is near than a brother who is far away"
Proverbs 27:10

The names that end up on the General Election ballot have almost universally been determined by a state's Primary earlier in the year. For partisan offices, many states advance the top vote-getting candidate for each official political party to face each other in November. For states with a "jungle Primary," the top two candidates independent of political party will square off in the General Election.

Although there are tactical refinements depending on the Primary process, you still have to choose a candidate to vote for. Since a Primary will generally have a larger slate to choose from, do you support: the candidate closest to your values or the one that is most electable and is not from the opposition political party?

If you're a person that stands on principle at all costs, you'll probably support a candidate that's like you, a Christian that is rock solid on all social and fiscal issues. However, more often than not those candidates are attractive to a dedicated Christian base, but have little appeal to the broader voting electorate. In fact, often they haven't had the years of preparation needed to cultivate name recognition, alliances with various groups, and the financial backing to be successful in a grueling campaign.

If you are more concerned about electability and keeping your political party in office, then a very electable candidate is more appealing to you even though you'll probably have to overlook some (if not many) of their positions on values that are important to you. Though this may be satisfying from a winning campaign standpoint, it may create conscience issues for you by appearing to support values inconsistent with your convictions (**Romans 14:23b**). It may also alienate you from committed Christians that want a clear Christian presence in public office.

Depending on the number of candidates, the split of votes between the above two approaches can easily result in a different person winning that's unacceptable to either group.

What would wisdom indicate in these situations? First, recognize that "compromise" is not a four-letter word. Like it or not, the nature of politics is that cooperation is often required to accomplish anything worthwhile. Second, Scripture indicates you have the freedom to make decisions that you think best, but you're not free to do so for any sinful purposes (**Galatians 5:13**). Third, Scripture does not command you to vote only for the perfect (in your eyes) candidate. God's common grace can use flawed individuals to fulfill His purposes, even though they may not be our first choice (**Proverbs 21:1**). However, it needs to be pointed out that if voting for a particular candidate would deeply violate your conscience before the Lord (i.e. they have major character flaws), then make the decision that will allow you to have a clear conscience (**Romans 14:23b**).

So, what should you do? Consider the possibility that the most effective approach, the one with the best opportunity to succeed, is supporting the candidate with good character that is closest to your most important policy positions (values), is also the most electable. This may not be an easy assessment to make, given a large field of candidates, but it's an important one given the need to sway enough of the electorate in the General Election.

In the long term, to keep such conscience/compromise situations from happening over-and-over again, prospective, highly-qualified candidates (**2 Timothy 2:14-26**) need to be groomed and resourced far in advance of any election. This type of commitment will help ensure the right candidate is the front-runner, becomes the most visible, and can garner the broadest electorate support.

PRINCIPLE #34
VOTING MAY ONLY PREVENT GREATER EVIL FROM OCCURRING

---

*"Take no part in the unfruitful works of darkness,
but instead expose them"*
Ephesians 5:11

It's a sad commentary on our times when an election comes down to choosing between two unacceptable candidates. This situation creates a moral dilemma for numerous people when they wonder how they can vote for the "lesser of two evils." After all, aren't you to avoid taking part in anything that's evil (**Ephesians 5:11**)?

The practical result of thinking this way is that many well-meaning believers will stay away from the polls altogether if the top of the ticket is an unworthy candidate; or they won't cast votes for any office unless there's clearly a good candidate in the race.

The problem with ignoring elections because of poor choices is that it improves the probability that the viler of two (or more) options will gain public office. This is true for every office you choose to not cast a vote.

The reality is that every candidate is a sinner, and there will never be a perfect candidate on any ballot (**Jeremiah 17:9**). And, in almost all cases, one candidate will be worse than the other. Even if two self-identified Christians are running against each other, both will be flawed in some way as each matures in the life-long sanctification process (**Philippians 1:6**).

So, how did we get to this point? You have to realize that voting is just the final step in a long process leading up to an election. Prospective candidates, to be viable, need to prepare for years before ever throwing their hat in the ring. They must invest time, treasure, and talent to gain support early on, and then network, gain alliances and endorsements, as well as secure strong financial commitments. But it doesn't stop there; they must generate name recognition, build trust with constituents, become articulate and discerning around a hostile media, and learn how to handle unprincipled opponents. All of this requires time to master.

Until a greater number of good people are willing to invest what it takes to run for office, many of the final voting choices you have to make will continue to be discouraging. However, a simple way to soften the conscience concern about voting for a lesser evil is to rephrase the decision as "voting to prevent the greater evil from occurring." It's more than simple semantics; this statement summarizes a clear moral imperative to minimize or limit the damage the vilest candidate would cause if they are elected.

Not surprisingly, voting this way can entail risk. Not from what the election outcome may be, but from other believers that disagree with your decision to vote at all. It comes down to both a wisdom issue (**1 Corinthians 10:23; Galatians 5:13**) and a conscience issue (**Romans 14:23b**), but it is not a "test of Christian orthodoxy" issue.

You need to be convinced in your mind that your voting decision is the correct one for you (**Romans 14:5**), and then be charitable towards those that would disagree based on their "principle" of not supporting any vile candidate no matter what the outcome will end up being.

The bottom line is that voting is the final step in a long process that led up to the particular candidates appearing on the ballot. To make those final choices more palatable in the future, maybe you or someone you know and trust needs to be encouraged to make the long-term commitment needed to eventually give voters a better choice.

PRINCIPLE #35

WE'RE ACCOUNTABLE FOR
EVERY CARELESS VOTE WE CAST

*"I tell you, on the day of judgment people will
give account for every careless word they speak"*
Matthew 12:36

You have a precious privilege and duty to vote to determine who will represent you and your values in the governance of your city, county, state, and country. When you vote you are legally expressing your will in a format that is equivalent to saying "Yes" or "No" in a court of law.

But more than any earthly court, there is a higher court that you are accountable to: the court of God. This should give you pause, particularly since you represent the Lord as His ambassador (**2 Corinthians 5:20a**) in the voting booth. This isn't an overstatement, since even careless words are of concern to Him (**Matthew 12:36**), and whatever we do in private or in public is important to Him (**Psalm 139:1-12**).

Voting is an expression of your values in the political arena. Your vote is not our spouse's, or a close friend's, or the message of some slick TV ad or random email, Twitter, Facebook, or other social media source. Every office listed on a ballot is asking your advice about who should occupy it; every proposition or initiative on the ballot is asking whether it should become a law or not. Every time you ignore an opportunity to make a good voting decision, you are wasting an opportunity to make a difference.

You're probably thinking you don't have the time or opportunity to invest the energy needed to evaluate all the candidates and proposed laws for yourself. That's understandable, but that's not acceptable!

How much time do you invest before you make a decision to buy some new clothes, or a fancy widget, or to enjoy a hobby, or deciding on the next great acquisition for a prized personal collection?

Those investments aren't wrong; in fact, Scripture says it's a blessing to enjoy those pursuits (**Ecclesiastes 2:24; 5:18-19; 8:15; 11:9**). But they don't have nearly the same impact on your life that bad laws (which last a long time) and corrupt politicians (that will be around for years) will have on you and your family.

So, what are you to do? First off, pray for wisdom and success in your investigation (**James 1:5**). Research a candidate's voting record if they're an incumbent, or their public statements, position papers and website if running for the first time. Attend public forums they're speaking at and ask them questions. Also, you can access information from organizations that are doing deep dives into a candidate's policy stances and any past voting record. If there's someone you trust that does methodical research into candidates and initiatives from at least a conservative perspective, use that information to supplement what you find out yourself.

Once you've done your research, you'll find yourself becoming an influencer of others, since very few will actually do what you're doing and will see you as a good source for help.

Ultimately, we know the Lord is in charge of every election, but we also know He uses His people (including you) to bring about political change intended for the good of us all (**Jeremiah 29:7; Proverbs 14:34**).

Bottom line, as with all life decisions, you're to be prudent and not careless, knowing that even with a secret ballot, God knows and sees it all (**Proverbs 15:3; Ecclesiastes 12:14**).

PART 7:
LOOKING AT CANDIDATES

E very candidate is going to have their individual strengths and weaknesses; and no candidate will ever be perfect. With that being said, there are a lot of things to consider when you decide who to support since your judgment is on the line. As much as possible, it's important to know a candidate's personal character, how they relate to others, how they handle personal attacks, whether they are serious about their personal faith, and if they are personally accountable to someone else in any meaningful way. Gaining insights into these factors may not be easy, but it will be well worth the effort in making your support decisions.

Principle #36

The World Values The Same Character Values You Do

"Moreover, he must be well thought of by outsiders,
so that he may not fall into disgrace, into a snare of the devil"
1 Timothy 3:7

Most companies will have a code of ethics, while governmental entities have standards of conduct. Whatever it's called, organizations will generally write down the types of character and behavior that's expected, and sometimes what will not be tolerated. It shouldn't surprise you that before the current irrational "wokeness" there was a lot of similarity in what those employment values were. Whether formal or not, these same expectations apply to every candidate seeking elective office, as well as everyone occupying a position of public influence.

Where do these "desirable" character trait expectations come from? They result from biblical character values of self-sacrifice that are in sharp contrast with worldly values of self-interest. Because of God's common grace, and specifically our nation's Christian legacy, honesty, integrity, faithfulness, diligence, transparency, humility, insightfulness, self-control, directness, wholesomeness, and initiative are important qualities to see in a leader (**Proverbs 8:14; 10:9; 12:22; 12:24; 28:20; Matthew 5:37; 1 Timothy 3:2-4; 2 Timothy 1:7; Titus 1:7-8; 1 Peter 5:5**).

Conversely, if a candidate is nuanced in what they say, difficult to pin down, plays to an audience, never admits fault, is hypocritical or prone to rashness, is vulgar, has a chaotic family life, or changes positions on critical issues without compelling reasons, then they're unworthy of support (**Proverbs 11:2; 20:17; 25:28; Ecclesiastes 5:2; Matthew 6:1; 7:5; Luke 16:15; Romans 16:18; Ephesians 5:3-4,6; etc.**). Even if their current policy positions generally line up with yours, it's not wise to trust these individuals to stand firm when pressured by fierce opposition or when self-interests take precedence (**James 1:8**).

Character traits are heart issues that reflect the quality of the person (**Luke 6:43-45**). They give an indicator of whether the person will do what they say they will do. As a Christian, you want to have confidence in the person you're supporting. So, just like elders and deacons are to first be tested (**1 Timothy 3:4,10**), so candidates should have some significant level of public and/or private track record verifying their true colors.

Even today, most people want someone that represents their interests to be trustworthy and teachable (**Proverbs 9:9; James 1:19**), whether they themselves are Christians or not. In point of fact, integrity may carry more significance for some of the voting public than actual policy positions. This is one reason why "character assassination" is such a common political tactic against an opponent. Destroy the reputation of a person in the public's eye, and that person will rarely recover.

How is this done? The ungodly political tactics of the world are clear: scream the same message loud and long enough and eventually many listeners will only see the attacked person through that filter (**2 Corinthians 2:11**). Calling someone a racist, homophobe, bigot, intolerant, hypocritical, a liar, extreme, out-of-the-mainstream, all without compelling proof (or any proof for that matter) is a vile tactic of Satan to destroy any thought that the candidate has the values (and character traits) we all want to see (**John 8:44; 2 Corinthians 10:4**).

Unfortunately, this type of despicable political warfare is common and must be exposed for what it is, disgusting (**Ephesians 5:11**). Whether ungodly attacks of that kind can be successfully countered or not, only time will tell. In the meantime, remember that ultimately the Lord will vindicate His chosen ones (**1 Peter 3:15-17**); in that we can place our hope and trust.

USING MINORITIES AS POLITICAL FODDER IS WICKED

"So God created man in his own image, in the image of God
he created him; male and female he created them"
Genesis 1:27

O ne of the favorite tactics of political adversaries is to divide and
conquer. By playing to secondary differences between people to
stir up controversy, they're able to champion themselves as their only
defenders. In reality, this grievance trafficking only feeds innate sinful
tendencies to be thought of as a victim. Politically exploitable differences
include social standing, education, race, ethnicity, income, sexual orien-
tation, or any other recognizable "distinction." Though real, these differences are not determinative, but they are useful for political gain since
most people will fall into one or more alleged "victim" categories.

What is determinative, and is far more important is something you know
from Scripture: everyone is created in the image of God (**Genesis 1:26-
27; Job 31:15**). The fact that every person has intrinsic value and dignity is lost on political difference-baiters. Being made in the image of
God overwhelms any superficial differences due to genetics, upbringing,
amount of initiative, or even "time and chance" that everyone experiences
(**Ecclesiastes 9:11**).

But there's more. From the beginning, God created the perfect family
design: one man and one woman married together and raising their children (**Genesis 2:24; Matthew 19:4-6; Ephesians 5:31**). This is the
greatest single factor for societal stability, and for the emotional, mental,
and economic health of the next generation. In contrast, anyone that seeks
to further divide people by promoting false constructs of marriage (i.e.

same-sex marriage) to garner minority support or appear to be non-judgmental will end up trivializing the effect of destructive behavioral habits and will eventually create unnecessary societal hardships and confusion.

How about education? Unions have a virtual stranglehold on most of the nation's primary and secondary educational institutions. Their core beliefs often include: activism over reasoned education, finding systemic racism over promoting equality of human dignity, and "system" imposed equity over hard work, initiative, and personal responsibility. In effect, children (another minority) are being turned against their parent's authority and values. Instead of being a temporary custodian in support of the parent (**1 Samuel 1:27-28; 2:11,26; 3:1a**), schools have often co-opted the parents' biblical role to train and equip their own children (**Deuteronomy 6:6-9; Psalm 127:3-5; Proverbs 22:6**).

Pick a topic, and any political group that zeros in on the sinful patterns of people and highlights alleged systemic discrimination independent of factual reality is creating far more problems than they are solving. However, from a Christian perspective all people are to be treated with dignity independent of their race or religion, income, or idiosyncrasies. This core biblical truth is in sharp contrast to the wickedness of politically-stoked class warfare!

A nation divided will not stand (**Mark 3:25**). When superficial differences become a major focus it's for one purpose, to use unsuspecting people to gain political power with no real intention to solve actual problems.

So, when you are evaluating candidates, listen very closely to what they say. Are they exploiting the differences in society to foment discontent and hatred (**Romans 16:17-18**)? Or are they highlighting what's consistent with God's design for a healthy society and promoting that design (**Matthew 6:28-33**) while showing compassion for those that are truly struggling (**Matthew 22:39**)? The former seek power by using smooth talk to play to sinful self-centeredness; the latter understands eternal values and what's best for everyone.

PRINCIPLE #38

A CANDIDATE CAN DO NO WRONG, UNTIL THEY'RE CHALLENGED BY SOMEONE ELSE

*"The one who states his case first seems right,
until the other comes and examines him"*
Proverbs 18:17

A favorite tactic of aggressive opponents is to paint their opposition in the darkest possible way, while portraying their candidate as being as pristine as the driven snow. The reason this is so common is because it tends to be very successful in swaying voters. Everyone wants to think they are fighting evil, while their person is clearly the perfect match for the job.

The problem is that we're all sinners (**Romans 3:11-12**), including those we support for public office. It's one thing to cut some slack for your candidate's weaknesses (skill set, aptitude, etc.), it's quite another to overlook moral failings or ethical lapses.

Rejecting what an opponent is saying without objectively assessing whether there's any merit to an accusation can be a recipe for disaster. In the worst case, you could become an inadvertent cheerleader for someone with major sin problems. The best case is that the accusations are unfounded and can be easily countered and then used as an indication of the dirty tactics being used (**2 Corinthians 10:3-4**); tactics that should be roundly condemned (**Ephesians 5:11**).

On the flip side, if there's something that needs to be addressed publically, it's best to be as objective about it as possible. For a Christian candidate this can be a public "teaching moment" to not only acknowledge past difficulties, but to explain why they were wrong, what was learned from them, and how they have changed as a result. This is something that most people can personally resonate with and appreciate, but a corrupt politician will never understand (**Proverbs 24:16; Romans 8:28**).

Likewise, believing that your candidate's opposition is evil incarnate in everything they do or say is probably just plain wrong. In fact, when we challenge someone's motives, we're in effect judging their heart, and that is something we need to be very careful about doing (**Matthew 7:1-5**).

We know the heart of an unregenerate person is vile (**Jeremiah 17:9**), but it's the rotting fruit of that heart concerning policy decisions and positions that's the clearest and most straightforward thing to challenge. Stooping to character assassination beyond objective facts about a person's life and decisions is tempting to do, but remember to whom we all will give an account of our lives (**Romans 14:12**). God will judge the secret things; we don't need to speculate (**Ecclesiastes 12:13-14**), particularly since speculation may only amount to gossip. And, as we all know, gossip is something that the Lord detests (**Proverbs 16:28; 21:23; James 1:26**).

Also, if you assume something about a candidate (your favorite one or the opposition) based solely on whether they self-identify as a Christian or not is probably unwise unless you know them personally and can testify to their true values and faith convictions. Otherwise, you may be unknowingly supporting a wolf in sheep's clothing (**Matthew 7:15-20; Hebrews 3:12; 6:4-6**). Third hand information from a trusted source about a candidates faith must be carefully considered and not necessarily taken at face value.

One final note, since we all have shortcomings (and sinful tendencies), it's not wrong to highlight a candidate's strengths without feeling obligated to spend an equal amount of time revealing their weaknesses. This falls into the category of wisdom depending upon the audience you're talking to, whether that audience is made up of personal friends, is a small group, a public forum, a news interview, or a personal blog (**Matthew 7:6**). In each of these situations you need to be circumspect and tailor the level of detail to the audience at hand.

PRINCIPLE #39

BEING A KING BREAKER CAN BE JUST AS IMPORTANT AS BEING A KING MAKER

"'God opposes the proud, but gives grace to the humble.'
Submit yourselves therefore to God. Resist the devil,
and he will flee from you."
James 4:6b-7

This is not a fun topic to cover. But reality tells us there are wolves in sheep's clothing in our midst (**Matthew 7:16-20**). A candidate for public office at any level will always try to win over a broad group of supporters. That's both understandable and good tactics. Unfortunately, someone that self-identifies as a Christian can easily win over gullible church-goers by just knowing the right lingo ("Christianese") to use.

Understandably, Christians want fellow Christians to occupy positions of public leadership. The problem occurs when there's a willingness to uncritically accept any semblance of faith and sincerity. You may be asking yourself if this is really a problem. Well, yes, it is! If the real person behind the words is actually against all that the biblical faith community stands for, that person is a deceiver and needs to be called out. Not only is this a serious matter of discernment, but it affects how precious election resources are going to be applied (i.e. finances, walking precincts, and voting).

Christians in general need to be "wise as serpents and innocent as doves" (**Matthew 10:16**) when it comes to vetting those that want support from the faith community. How mature and deep is the candidate's faith; are they strong on sanctify of life issues, marriage and family, and the limited role of governments; are they a member of a Christ-honoring and Bible-preaching church? Also, are they personally accountable to anyone, and are they willing to take a stand publically on values critical to Christians?

Unfortunately, Christians can be very naïve in political matters, and want to assume the best when someone claims to be a "person of faith." That term, left unchallenged, can be cover for a lot of things, including non-biblical values and even heresy.

Biblically, if a candidate claims to be a believer, then they should be able to convincingly talk about their faith. Relative to positions on issues, they need to be confronted biblically (**Matthew 18:15-17**) about any unacceptable stances. If either of these two probes shows very disconcerting results, then publically warning the wider community may be called for (**Ephesians 5:11**). Scripture is clear, someone that professes to know God, yet their works and values indicate otherwise are unfit for any good work (**Titus 1:16**).

This may sound extreme, but remember that once a person is elected to public office and becomes an incumbent, they're in a much stronger position the next time around. Also, preventing a wolf from being elected the first time may prevent them from gaining higher office in the future where they can have even more destructive influence.

Being a "king breaker" is not a desirable thing to be, but it's part of the Christian community doing its homework to actually help godly leaders get elected, and not allow them to be edged out by smooth-talking hypocrites (**2 Timothy 3:5**).

So how does a person vote if the candidate "on their side" is a wolf in sheep's clothing and the other opponent is unacceptable?

Generally, it's wise to vote to prevent the greater evil from occurring. However, in the case of a known wolf and a vile opponent, your conscience may dictate not voting for that position at all. Others may feel free to vote for a "reasonable" candidate if they're not claiming to be a Christian. In either case, the goal is to honor the name of Christ, and then begin planning for the next election cycle.

PRINCIPLE #40
NEVER LEAVE A CHRISTIAN IN PUBLIC OFFICE TO FEND FOR THEMSELVES

*"Therefore encourage one another and
build one another up, just as you are doing"*
1 Thessalonians 5:11

*"First of all, then, I urge that supplications, prayers,
intercessions, and thanksgivings be made for all people, for kings
and all who are in high positions, that we may lead a peaceful
and quiet life, godly and dignified in every way"*
1 Timothy 2:1-2

I t's common to think that successful people have it all together. The higher the position of influence, the less accessible a person generally is, and the more they tend to be idolized by their supporters. Those in authority indeed have greater access to information and resources to better understand issues, but they're also exposed to a broader range of temptations.

Scripture says for believers to pray for each other (**Ephesians 6:18**), but it's interesting to see an urgency expressed concerning prayer for government leadership (**1 Timothy 2:1-2**). One reason is that they have so much power over those they govern, but another is the nature of the temptations they experience. Do we really think Christians will never compromise here and there, or succumb to cutting corners even though there may be some ethical issues, or even rationalize a terrible decision because they think the end result "is for a greater good" and will be blessed? Consider your life; how successful have you been?

A tendency among Christians is to relax after a campaign when "their guy or gal" gets into office. A certain "fire and forget" attitude can develop that thinks things are now OK. The truth of the matter is that once a believer gets into office, there should be even more prayer for them, more encouragement given to them to stay the course, and yes more accountability is needed.

If pastors can succumb to sexual temptation, or the lure of easy church financial access, or the abuse of their power, why would we think that Christian politicians would be sin-proof given the even greater breadth and depth of possible compromises available to them (**James 1:12-15**)?

One of the best things that can be done for believers in public office (or any position of governmental influence) is to encourage them to be accountable to a mature believer that will be direct about both professional and personal matters. Is there someone in their life that's willing to ask them specific, sensitive questions to find out how they're really doing and what they're struggling with? How do they spend their spare time, is there someone that they find themselves particularly attracted to, are they hiring staff based on looks rather than qualifications, are there campaign financial donations available from dubious organizations or people that will expect something in return? The list could go on and on.

An older, spiritually mature friend may be a good person to provide some accountability (**Proverbs 18:24**), as could other seasoned politicians that have proven themselves in this uniquely challenging environment. It will take someone with good insights that is also an encourager and can build up and not just be critical (**1 Thessalonians 5:11**). Whether you're the person that could become that source of help or not, you still need to be an encourager to the one in office – giving sincere thanks when good decisions are made, and gentle reproof when clearly bad ones are made (**Galatians 6:1**).

The greater the responsibility someone has, the greater the need for some level of accountability (**Proverbs 27:17; Ephesians 4:25; James 5:19-20**). This is true in anyone's personal life, in their professional life, and clearly in any political life.

PART 8:
BEING A CANDIDATE

Running for elective office is one of the most challenging pursuits a person can take on. Not only can it be frustrating, exciting, rewarding, costly and draining, but it will probably bring all your character flaws and strengths into the light of day depending on the importance of the office you want to occupy. Do you have a "past", are you used to being pummeled with "gotcha" questions, are you running for the right reasons, are you a different person in public than you are in private, can you admit fault? These are all good questions to ask yourself as you navigate the labyrinth of political pursuits.

Principle #41

Running For Office Takes More Than Just Showing Up

"Do you see a man skillful in his work? He will stand before kings; he will not stand before obscure men"
Proverbs 22:29

Running for office, any office, takes hard work. It also takes passion, money, interpersonal, management, and administrative skills, a lot of detailed planning, a broad support base, an articulate message, and far more time than ever anticipated.

Why is this important to say? Because Christians tend to be naive about political realities and assume the Lord will provide. To want to be the "white knight" that swoops in at the 11th hour to save the day is an exciting dream, but it can also be foolhardy and very presumptuous towards God and reality (**James 4:13-14**).

I know what you're thinking right now: "Oh you of little faith" (**Matthew 6:30**). But wait a minute, God promises to meet your daily needs (**Matthew 6:25-33**), He doesn't promise to fulfill your wild dreams or bless your foolish desires. You may think that running for political office is a direct calling from God and He is duty-bound to bless your campaign; but your decision to run is merely exercising your liberty to seek to be a blessing to our community (**Jeremiah 29:7**).

Occupying elective office is a high privilege since you serve God first (**1 Corinthians 10:31**) and then those you represent (**Romans 13:4a**). Responsibilities of this sort are never to be taken lightly; instead, they must be prayerfully and adequately prepared and fought for.

Preparation for a campaign and then to be effective once in office will probably take years of diligent work. Without that preparation, one of two things will happen: either you won't be elected because you built your campaign on sand (**Matthew 7:26-27**), or if elected you may find yourself incompetent to exercise the authority entrusted to you. Neither of these outcomes, by the way, honors the Lord.

Diligence and persistence are far more likely to yield success than thinking you have all the right answers and just assuming the best. That's the message of **Proverbs 22:29**, those that are skilled will be recognized for their competence and supported. Those that rely on a miracle to happen to gain public office are just setting themselves up for failure, even if they are the most professionally qualified candidate (**Proverbs 24:30-34**). In fact, just putting all your trust in the Lord and not working incredibly hard may show more of a prideful heart that is seeking recognition instead of a passion to pursue God-honoring public ministry.

I know there are rare examples of someone bursting on the scene and "saving the day" for the Lord against all odds (**Ecclesiastes 9:11**). I'm sure there are incredibly unusual circumstances that probably made that possible. But history, experience, and thousands of futile election campaigns tell a different story.

The bottom line: plan, prepare, and show up ready to work. Above all, seek the Lord's blessing on your labors and not just His blessing because you have the right intentions.

PRINCIPLE #42
YOU DON'T HAVE TO SHARE THE GOSPEL IN EVERY SPEECH

"Behold, I am sending you out as sheep in the midst of wolves, so be wise as serpents and innocent as doves"
Matthew 10:16

For a Christian, the gospel is everything. That's why we're engaged in politics: to protect our religious right to openly proclaim and live out God's Word, and to help implement Christ-honoring, godly principles for the common good of everyone.

But like evangelizing, time and place are important. In other words, you need to know your audience.

It's one thing to share your faith with a group of friends or with someone that needs to hear the message of salvation. It's quite another, however, to think you're obligated to give the gospel message every time you give a political presentation or interview. In large gatherings that want to hear what your policy positions are, it's easy to slip into a comfortable mode of attributing everything to the Lord and the importance of His Word in your life.

For believers, that will be an encouragement to them, since you're "standing tall for Jesus." But for those that are not Christians, and also for any adversarial press that may be present, you have just given them an angle to reject anything else you say. In fact, quotes lifted out of context will probably be used over and over again to discredit you as a religious zealot, a narrow-minded bumpkin, an out-of-touch Neanderthal; you know the routine.

There will be plenty of times to share how the gospel continues to mature your life to please God. The point of **Matthew 10:16**, however, is that you are not obligated to throw your pearls before swine (**Matthew 7:6**), so you need to be wise and know who you're talking to and what's needed at any given time.

Does this mean you don't publically answer questions about your faith? You can answer, but you can also be circumspect about specifics that could otherwise be easily manipulated and misrepresented. This takes practice, but it's an important skill to develop if you're going to be in the public eye. In effect, don't give ammunition to your enemy if you don't have to.

Obviously, your faith will be a factor in any political environment. But remember that there will be many opportunities to show the depth and breadth of your convictions other than directly to a TV camera. When those occasions occur, a simple attribution to God may be sufficient for the time being. Your life, your decisions, and a demonstrated prioritization of your family will always show your biblical priorities are right.

So when can you share? You can discuss faith and truth with groups that are aligned with Christian values, knowing they will spread the word to like-minded folks about your convictions. Also, sharing the gospel and its hold on you with your trusted advisors will demonstrate where your heart is, where you draw strength from, and to Whom you look for favor. It will also set the backdrop for all future campaign and public office decisions that need to be made (**Proverbs 3:5-6**).

Bottom line: you proclaim truth when you refuse to slander, lie, cheat, or misrepresent for any reason (**Exodus 20:16; Proverbs 12:22; James 4:17**) since you answer to a higher authority than the electorate. You also proclaim the gospel when you publically give thanks to God, no matter how short a statement it is. It doesn't have to be elaborate or profound. But by just mentioning "God" you're already set apart because you acknowledge that a divine nature exists. What setting will be appropriate to go beyond that simple statement will take wisdom and discernment, the very thing God promises to provide in abundance if you ask Him for it (**James 1:5**).

Principle #43

Nothing Is Ever, Really, Off The Record

"Let no corrupting talk come out of your mouths,
but only such as is good for building up, as fits the occasion,
that it may give grace to those who hear"
Ephesians 4:29

You're never alone: even if there's nobody around, the Lord hears every word you speak! In fact, He even knows what you're thinking (**Psalm 139:1-2**). Always keeping that in mind should give you pause whenever you open your mouth or you let your mind wander carelessly.

Ungodly words are always destructive (**Matthew 12:36; James 3:6-8**), and will never accomplish godly purposes. Everyone that speaks in the public arena better understand quickly that their words can carry weight far beyond the immediate context. It's hard enough to effectively communicate cogent and consistent thoughts, it's even more difficult to try to prevent your words from being taken out of context and then used against you (**Psalm 56:5**).

Since that's the case in formal and semi-formal settings, it's easy to "let down" and be less careful in informal settings with friends, family, and those we work closely with. But if you're different in informal settings than formal ones, which person is the real "you"? If you use course language, innuendo, swearing, or the caveat "I'll be honest with you" language when you think you're safe from the public eye, then maybe your heart isn't quite right by trying to falsely project a different public persona (**Matthew 23:28**). The reality is that what you say and how you say it in less threatening environments will reveal more about your heart, and who you really are, than at any other times (**Matthew 15:18**).

Because the words you speak are so important, most of an entire book of the Bible (**James**) is written to warn you about the use of your tongue. So, besides committing a lot of that book to memory, what else should you do?

First, set an example wherever you are, and be consistent. Your nature has been changed by the redemptive work of Christ in your life. You don't have to play word games to make others think you're someone you aren't. You don't have to keep in mind which of two sides of your nature to present depending upon the circumstances. You are a Christian at all times (**1 Corinthians 10:31-32**), and you need to be mature, not hypocritical or "salty" or offensive (**Colossians 4:6**), but always be wise in the words you use (**Ephesians 4:29**).

Second, besides reminding yourself that the Lord is with you wherever you are, a good way to keep your tongue in check is to imagine an "open" or "hot" microphone is in your face and recording everything. Not only is that probably convicting already, but what if those recordings are then broadcast on the nightly news for your family, your friends, and the entire world to hear (**Ecclesiastes 10:20**)? If that makes you uncomfortable, think about what you're saying, who you're talking about, and how you're saying it.

Finally, it's also good to be accountable to others. If you're married, does your spouse sense anything out of whack in how you talk in public compared to how you are in private? Do any of your close friends detect two (or more) different people depending upon the circumstances? If they can, the public will eventually notice it also.

Ultimately, your whole life is "on the record" with the Lord. So, bridle your tongue for your sake, the sake of your hearers, and most certainly for the sake of the Lord that you want to honor (**2 Timothy 2:21**).

PRINCIPLE #44
GOSSIP IS SIN, NO MATTER HOW IMPORTANT AN ELECTION

"If anyone thinks he is religious and does not bridle his tongue but deceives his heart, this person's religion is worthless"
James 1:26

Have you ever received damaging information about someone that was too good to be true? More often than not it's probably false. It may be consistent with what you want to believe; you may be tempted to send it to all your friends as a "gotcha" on a vile opposition candidate; or you may use it out of revenge for what the "other side" wrongly said about you or "your candidate."

Unfortunately, we all can have itching ears, particularly when it comes to gaining some political advantage in a campaign that's intense and close. The question is: what's the right thing to do?

The world uses lies, distortions, misrepresentations, intimidation, accusations, and any number of other tactics to destroy its opposition. Those tactics are ungodly, but not unexpected (**2 Corinthians 2:11**). You, however, are God's ambassador in this world (**2 Corinthians 5:20a**), and are privileged to represent Christ in everything you do. The most important tactics available to you are spiritual in nature (**2 Corinthians 10:4**) and don't require the use of distasteful, sleazy, or questionable information to manipulate others to support your side.

So, how do we know when some article or statement or email is true or false in this age of fake news and a flood of social media and late-breaking revelations? The first indicator is if the story is from a reputable source, or references are provided that can be verified. Even then, information can be slanted to paint an unwarranted picture (or to impugn motives) contrary to an otherwise objective account.

If you receive an unsourced piece of salacious material, it's best to delete it and not forward it to anyone else unless you can credibly check its validity. Remember, your reputation is on the line whenever you say or send or televise anything to someone else. And, once your credibility is tainted, your personal effectiveness is also damaged (**Proverbs 22:1; Ecclesiastes 7:1a**).

Now, you may be thinking: "But this is warfare! Didn't Old Testament Israel lie in warfare?" In the Old Testament, military deception was not only condoned, it was prescribed by the LORD for use by the Israelites towards their enemies (**Joshua 8:1-23; Judges 7:1-22**). In life-death circumstances, providing information (or more accurately an appearance) that is misinterpreted by an enemy is not forbidden. What is sinful, however, is viciously lying to harm someone else (**Exodus 20:16**), or flagrantly misrepresenting a situation in order to maliciously destroy another person. Lying is a heart issue that emanates from Satan, the father of lies (**John 8:44**) and not from Jesus Christ the source of all truth (**John 14:6**).

The worldly heart doesn't care about truth; it is only concerned about winning and using any means necessary to do so. But the people of God answer to a higher authority (**Romans 14:12**), and will be rewarded accordingly (**Romans 2:6-11**). No matter how tempting late "game-changer" stories are, gossip is vile (**Exodus 20:16; 23:1; Proverbs 10:18; 17:4; 18:8; 19:5**) and needs to be avoided for your sake, and ultimately for the sake of your witness for the gospel of Jesus Christ.

Principle #45

Know How To Answer Unfounded Accusations

"Answer not a fool according to his folly, lest you be like him yourself. Answer a fool according to his folly, lest he be wise in his own eyes"
Proverbs 26:4-5

A favorite tactic of an unscrupulous politician is to denigrate their opposition by labeling them with intentionally inflammatory terms. This not only energizes their base, but it puts opponents on the defensive to try to correct a false characterization.

Unfortunately, it's difficult to effectively counter vile, unfounded accusations like being called a racist, a homophobe, a religious zealot (or fanatic), or a far-out extremist. It's never going to be enough to just deny being what those terms imply, and that's the point of the attacks. You will use up precious time trying to prove these claims are false while looking defensive in doing so, and all the while not focusing on the political issues at hand. So, what are you to do?

If you take the bait, become defensive, and answer with something like: "I never did anything like that" or "I'm not," you open yourself up to being challenged to prove your assertions. It's far easier to prove something happened than to prove something never happened, and adversaries know this.

Scripture gives at least four approaches in response to personal attacks. Depending on the question, the first is to just give a simple "Yes" or "No" answer and leave it at that (**Matthew 5:37**). Going beyond that may only serve to legitimize the question by treating it like it really was a valid issue to bring up.

The second possible response was used by Jesus numerous times: answer a question by asking a question (**Matthew 9:14-15; 15:1-3; 17:24-26; 26:6-10; Mark 10:2-3; Luke 2:48-49; 10: 25-26**; etc.). If phrased well, this can put the onus back on the challenger to prove their claim, or show the incompetence of the reporter for not investigating the assertion and instead aiding and abetting a lie.

Another approach is to deflect and refer a reporter (or challenger) to those that know you the best for the longest period of time, and let them answer for you (**Proverbs 27:2**). This makes the accuser do the work they should have done to begin with and doesn't waste your valuable time. Jesus did this by referring to His works that testified (served as a witness) about Him (**John 10:24-26**).

Finally, if a serious question concerning your character or your past decisions and statements is addressed in a setting that's conducive to being addressed at length, you can take the time to talk it through. In these environments, the heart of the issue can be exposed: liars will say anything to try and destroy an opponent. When that tactic is being used, it needs to be confronted for the evil that it is (**Exodus 20:16; Ephesians 5:11**).

When the substance of policy positions cannot win the day, character assassination is the tool of choice for those that are unscrupulous. In a real sense, calling others detestable names is often a projection of one's own corrupt character, a character consistent with the father of all lies (**John 8:44**). When these attacks occur, the responsibility needs to be put back on the attacker to prove that their claims are true, without you having to waste time countering every wild statement or speculation that is made against you.

When to fight back, and how to answer accusations requires great wisdom and practice. But fortunately for you, wisdom is exactly what the Lord promises to provide if you sincerely ask for it (**Proverbs 26:4-5; James 1:5**).

Principle #46
Are You Able To Admit Fault?

"Whoever conceals his transgressions will not prosper,
but he who confesses and forsakes them will obtain mercy"
Proverbs 28:13

A n unwritten rule in worldly politics is to never admit fault and to paint everything the opponent says or does as purely evil. Is this an overstatement? Consider the typical campaign ads that you've seen on TV, or received in the mail or electronically. Candidate A claims Candidate B can literally do nothing right in word or deed, but Candidate A is pure and perfect in everything they do. And, these claims become even more strident and shocking as the election draws closer.

But, what about you; what are you going to do when you're attacked personally?

If attacks against you are just lying smears to try to discredit you for things in the past or present, you have every right to defend yourself and call out the lies (**John 8:45-46; Acts 25:9-12**). But what happens if you did do something wrong and the opposition runs wild with it? Your immediate response will probably be to become defensive, want to trivialize the significance, or even to outright deny whatever happened.

If what you did was an oversight or mistake, you need to deal with it quickly and objectively. But, if you were willfully sinful, as a Christian you answer to a higher authority that will not bless hidden sin (**Numbers 32:23; Proverbs 28:13**). In admitting what you've done, you have an opportunity to show your redeemed character and confess the wrong, openly, and without excuse. In doing this you'll need to trust the Lord for whatever outcome may occur after that. But, depending on how significant the issue, you also may need to do some deep soul-searching to determine if you really should be pursuing elective office, which requires a lot of public and private trust.

We've all done things in the past that we're not proud of. If you're seeking elective office you may want to admit up front what you've done in the past, while being appropriately circumspect. This is a biblical tactic that can disarm your opponents before opposition research finds and then distorts what really happened (**Proverbs 28:13**).

As a Christian, we have an incredible advantage over the ungodly; we can be open about our failings (**James 5:16**). When we are, we have a platform to speak to eternal truths that will touch many other people personally. By admitting prior sins, we can use our life to illustrate what is right and wrong behavior (**Matthew 7:13-14**). By talking about forgiveness, we can point to the ultimate source of forgiveness: God the Father through Jesus Christ (**1 John 1:9**), as well as the need to be reconciled to whomever we've wronged (**Matthew 5:23-26**).

Also, by being transparent we can talk about the lessons we've learned from our past, how those lessons have impacted our life (**Hebrews 12:11**), and how we make decisions as a result of those failings. Since people of all persuasions can understand these types of personal issues that make you more relatable to them, your opposition may suddenly become more reluctant to bring your past up.

Bottom line: as with all of life, circumstances will vary for each situation and wisdom from the Lord will need to be sought (**James 1:5**). But always remember that the Lord will provide you with the answer as to what to do that will benefit you and honor Him (**1 Corinthians 10:13**). We all are sinners, but our mighty Lord is merciful (**1 John 1:9-10**).

PRINCIPLE #47
ARE YOU A GLORY HOUND?

"It is not good to eat much honey,
nor is it glorious to seek one's own glory"
Proverbs 25:27

If you're running for office, you "are" the center of attention. You're the one that the campaign is all about, and the one that needs to be in the public's eye in as many ways as possible to garner as many votes as possible.

As more and more people begin to encourage you, the atmosphere will become that much more intoxicating. And, not surprisingly, being the center of attention can easily feed your pride. As that happens, you'd better force yourself to constantly remember that you are where you are because of the Lord; as was the case with Esther (**Esther 4:13-14**). And, just as God hates a prideful heart (**Proverbs 8:13; 16:5,18; 29:23; James 4:6**), He can just as easily remove you from your place of prominence, or grant you success in your political pursuits (**Psalm 75:6-7; Daniel 2:21**).

Besides forgetting about the Lord, there's a second temptation. You may begin to really believe that you are the center of everything and that everything and everybody else is less important and revolves around you. As a Christian, the example of Christ should be constantly in your mind. He gave up everything for the sake of others (**Philippians 2:5-11**), and you're called to have the same humility to count others as more significant than yourself (**Philippians 2:3**).

The world loves a winner (**1 Corinthians 9:24**), but at what cost? The world admires leaders that are aggressive, self-confident, powerful, assertive, seemingly invincible, and have all the right answers. You, however, are certainly called to be competent (**Proverbs 22:29**), but not the "be-all and end-all" of everything political. Unlike the world, you're to be sincerely gracious (**Ephesians 4:32; Colossians 3:12**), thankful (**1 Thessalonians 5:18**), patient (**Galatians 5:22**), generous with praise, an encourager to others (**Ephesians 4:29; 1 Thessalonians 5:11**), and not become a glory hound (**Proverbs 25:27**).

Being "other-oriented" also includes acknowledging (publically and privately) the hard work (and resources) that others have put in to help you be successful. You really can't do it all yourself, and most of the important work being done will be by volunteers. And yes, they need to be encouraged as much as you do. In fact, being grateful and also objective about yourself (**Romans 12:3**) will go a long way to building commitment from others, and having them openly speak well of you instead of you trying to hog credit for everything (**Proverbs 27:2**).

A dramatic biblical account of what happened to King Herod Agrippa I is a good one to keep in mind when we start to think of ourselves more highly than we should. In **Acts 12:21-23**, King Agrippa gave an oration to a crowd, and was praised by them as if he were not a man, but a god. His accepting that adoration (glory) without turning it back towards the true and living God resulted in his immediate death and being eaten by worms!

The bottom line is that there is only One that deserves glory, and that is the Lord (**Isaiah 48:11**). Seeking glory for yourself is part of your old nature (**Proverbs 25:27**), not the new one that the Lord has given you through redeeming you at a great price (**2 Corinthians 5:17**).

PART 9:
TACTICAL ISSUES

S etting goals that are achievable is one thing; how you go about
achieving those goals will say a lot about who you are and how you
relate to those around you. Are you naive, are you willing to defer to the
judgment of others, are you a "win at all costs" type of person, or are you
the type that always wants to stay above the fray? For political success, you
will need to have a large skill set, as well as a pretty good understanding of
people in general. Do you think you have that?

PRINCIPLE #48

BE WILLING TO DEFER ON TACTICAL APPROACHES WHENEVER POSSIBLE

*"Having gifts that differ according to
the grace given to us, let us use them"*
Romans 12:6a

Politics has it all: drama, insights, challenges, uncertainties, friends, enemies, unknowns, heartaches, sleepless nights, joys, and a lot of opinions and talk. It also has a lot of decisions that have to be assessed, reassessed, and changed if necessary. To reach any strategic goal, the use of the right tactics is crucial to being able to carry the day. Since everybody has opinions, the question often comes down to deciding which tactics are best.

Campaigns to elect someone else, or yourself for that matter, rely on a lot of hard work, experience, and an understanding of current electorate dynamics. If you fancy yourself as a master strategist with a lot of prior success under your belt in the "normal" world of employment, be prepared for a surprise. What may work in corporate environments may not be directly applicable for a fickle, emotionally-infused political battle. It doesn't mean your opinions and insights aren't valuable, but they may not be as germane as you think they are.

Do a self-evaluation. If you aren't flexible and adaptable, you may have a problem with your pride (**Proverbs 12:15; 19:20-21; Romans 12:3**). If successful leaders throughout history relied on wise counsel to be successful, why would it be any different for you (**Proverbs 11:14; 15:22**)? Scripture says you're to always be teachable (**Proverbs 9:9**); in time, you will become the teacher if you are first a good student.

Given the above, it's still good to not just accept what others say without questioning the how and why of what's happening. A good thing to ask yourself, and those you are campaigning with, is whether the approach being followed is immoral, illegal, or unethical. If it is any of those things, then it should be challenged since it reflects on you, whether you're the candidate or not. After all, you serve a mighty God, the One that holds your future and the election outcome in His hands. Buying into the tactics used by the world (i.e. ungodly) should never be expected to bring God's blessings (**2 Corinthians 10:3-5**).

Experience is a great teacher, and learning from others that have been involved with politics for a long time will be more valuable than gold (**Proverbs 8:10-11; 16:16**). That doesn't mean, however, that something new can't be tried, even if it's unorthodox. After all, don't forget the novel tactics employed by Gideon (**Judges 7:1-22**) that won the battle against Midian.

It's also OK to be shrewd and clever in developing and implementing campaign tactics (**Matthew 10:16; Romans 16:19**). But that should never be a cover to justify ungodly means that would bring discredit on you.

At the end of the day, tactics may be new, old, or just different, but they need to be godly and not give a questionable impression to those that are working with or for you. Anything else needs to be questioned and modified to ensure you're able to remain above reproach (**Titus 1:7a**).

PRINCIPLE #49

COMPROMISE IS NOT A FOUR-LETTER WORD

*"For you were called to freedom, brothers. Only do not
use your freedom as an opportunity for the flesh,
but through love serve one another"*
Galatians 5:13

Compromise is one of those terms that can either describe great success in trying to accomplish something or be used as a pejorative to condemn somebody.

In our everyday life, compromise is a routine matter of maturely balancing the desires or needs of people. However, in the hotly-contested area of politics it's easy to get caught up in "winning" at all costs and not giving an inch to the other side. This makes sense if fundamental, life-impacting decisions are involved, but the reality is that there are very few of those stark black-and-white situations in governance. In fact, the vast majority of decisions are routine matters that are not earth-shattering, though they will still be important.

What this means in practical terms is that unless conservative (or conservative-leaning) politicians are the voting majority in any governing body, then negotiations, reasoning, and presentation of fact-based information are the primary tools used to try and limit the amount of damage the other side of the political spectrum can inflict (whether their goals are well-meaning or not). While trying to minimize the impact, it will take real skill to gain as much agreement as possible in areas that are important for furthering conservative principles.

When in the legislative minority, the best situation will be when a common goal can be agreed to, and the means to get there are mutually acceptable to both sides. However, the most controversial areas between the political left and right (abortion, LGBTQ rights, debt, role of government, etc.) will have both divergent goals and probably little, if anything, in common. Any progress under these conditions will be very difficult, if not impossible to gain. These situations will require a firm, principled stand with a clear "Yes" or "No" as you answer to the Lord in an area that Scripture is very clear about (**Matthew 5:37**). The good news is that the opportunity to publically defend what you think is right and why, may actually end up having far more impact than you ever imagined (**Isaiah 55:11; Matthew 5:13-16**). Being articulate during those times can and has been used by the Lord to sway even hardened public opinions (**Proverbs 25:15**). In addition, speaking against horrible proposals in a public meeting or hearing will place the truth you present into the public record for later reference.

Where legislative goals are questionable, a conservative minority is often left with trying to minimize the most glaring problem areas by making them as publicly visible as possible. In rare cases of poor legislation it may be prudent to provide bi-partisan support to gain broader support for other, more desirable legislation later. This type of "compromise" requires a great amount of wisdom (**James 1:5**), and an ability to explain decisions to a Christian community that will probably be the most vocal to condemn perceived compromise of any type.

Building trust with fellow believers, and convincing them that you are gaining as much as possible given a very difficult situation, is going to be hard to do. The key is to show how your freedom to negotiate and make decisions is needed, and that you're not doing so for reasons of personal gain, but rather to further biblical values (**Galatians 5:13**).

The best solution is to prevent having to put conservative Christians in a legislative minority position to begin with. Until that happens, wise compromise may be the best that is possible unless the Lord provides a better way (**1 Corinthians 10:13**).

PRINCIPLE #50

IF YOU STAND ON PRINCIPLE TO THE POINT OF INACTION, YOU BECOME PART OF THE PROBLEM

*"Therefore let us not pass judgment on one
another any longer, but rather decide never to put a
stumbling block or hindrance in the way of a brother"*
Romans 14:13

I f you're a "principlist" type of person, God's Word is your gold standard to scrutinize every political decision (**Psalm 119:105; Proverbs 30:5; Romans 15:4**). By keeping our core values always in the forefront, you make sure Christians can't easily ignore them, or make a decision out of pure expediency. These are good traits to have, especially since they remind other believers that this truly is spiritual warfare, and spiritual weapons are needed (**2 Corinthians 10:4-5**).

On the other hand, "bending" may not be in your vocabulary if you believe every application of God's truth is tantamount to defending God's honor. If this is you, then it wouldn't be surprising if others see you as strident, harsh, narrow-minded, or worse yet, insufferable. The question you need to answer is whether standing on principle to the point of creating divisiveness is a godly thing to do when political work by its nature is compromise and negotiation with a wide range of people, both believers and non-believers (**Proverbs 16:2**).

We know that to the unbelieving world we're the aroma of death because we belong to Jesus Christ (**2 Corinthians 2:15-16**). In the major political battles in our nation, it's clear there are many that despise biblical values relating to life, marriage, sexuality, and any limitations on the role of governments. And, unless the Lord intervenes and softens hearts, there's little potential to move that segment toward accepting our values as the right ones. However, on the conservative side of the political divide there can be real victories in promoting our values when enough people are convinced to contribute time, treasure, and talent in electing godly leaders to public office and supporting the passage of good legislation and policies.

If biblical Christians were the overwhelming number of citizens participating in the political process, a "principlist" could accomplish an incredible amount. But the reality is that Christians with a biblical worldview are generally a small percentage of those engaged in the battle. Given that, anyone splitting off a group of like-minded purists that "take no prisoners," only helps ensure defeat at the ballot box when the vote is fragmented. This in turn minimizes any political pressure that could otherwise be applied for good legislation.

Though you may be taking the noble high ground position, the reality is that trying to apply God's perfection in a sinful world for the common good requires application of wisdom with tactical insight, and yes, even compromise (**Luke 14:31-32**). Being inflexible, particularly in areas that may not be clearly and unambiguously addressed by Scripture, may serve to salve your conscience but doom any political progress from happening if you end up impacting enough other people.

The bottom line is that if you find yourself incapable of constructively working on political campaigns, or that your conscience is continually provoked (**Romans 14:23b**), it may be best to remove yourself from the battle. Scripture warns about arguing over words (**2 Timothy 2:14**), which only ruins the hearers. Being an effective promoter of salt and light (**Matthew 5:13-16**) will take a lot of time and understanding. And, even though you may be completely right in what you're promoting, you need to be very careful that you are not coming across as self-righteous or using "the perfect" as an excuse to actually do nothing.

PRINCIPLE #51
GODLY GOALS CAN NEVER JUSTIFY THE USE OF UNGODLY MEANS

"For though we walk in the flesh, we are not waging war according to the flesh. For the weapons of our warfare are not of the flesh but have divine power to destroy strongholds. We destroy arguments and every lofty opinion raised against the knowledge of God, and take every thought captive to obey Christ"
2 Corinthians 10:3-5

It's easy to naively accept the old saying: "All's fair in love and war," particularly since the philosophy behind this secular proverb encapsulates so much of the hard-hitting politics of our day. In effect, this phrase says it's OK to use any means necessary to accomplish a goal, whether that goal is a good one or not.

The problem with this thinking is at least two-fold. First, the goal itself should be questioned as to whether it's worthy of significant support. Secondly, even if the goal seems noble, virtually any ungodly tactic can be justified to accomplish that goal, no matter how shameful the tactics may be.

For a Christian, the "ends-justify-the means" mentality is not an option if it entails ungodly means. We answer to a higher authority (**Matthew 12:36**), not to the bottom line of a political win-loss record.

For sure, there are many nuances of political battle that are clever, impactful, ethical, and effective. Even in Old Testament warfare, deception was a tactic the Lord allowed Gideon to use against Israel's enemies (**Judges 7:1-23**). But even that deception was no more than giving the appearance of a greater armed force than was really there. That is far removed from today's deceit, lying, threats, unfounded character assassination, false reporting, false testimony, false "fact-checking", social and news media censorship, and smear campaigns that are used to detract from policy issues and utterly destroy the reputation (and even family) of an opponent. These means to an end are wicked, and should be exposed as the disgraceful, disgusting tactics that they are (**Ephesians 5:11**).

For the Christian, we have tremendous freedom for action, but not to employ tactics that would bring dishonor on the name of our Savior (**Galatians 5:13**). Whether you are a candidate for elective or appointive office, or supporting a candidate; whether you are fighting for a piece of legislation or against one, you are to be above reproach in everything you do (**1 Peter 3:15-17**).

The Apostle Paul faced a similar question about goals and means when he asked: "Are we to continue in sin that grace may abound" (**Romans 6:1**)? His unequivocal response: "By no means!" (**Romans 6:2**). His point is clear: we don't sin to accomplish "good results."

Although typical political tactics can be sophisticated and multi-faceted, you also have several other weapons at your disposal: prayer, reasoning, and truth (**2 Corinthians 10:3-5**). Remember, spiritual warfare is the background to all political warfare, so spiritual weapons are just as (if not more) critical as any other weapon.

Finally, if your role is to influence those that are not yet convinced of the rightness of your fight, you can win many over by your gentle (yet firm) answers to questions and challenges (**Proverbs 15:1**). By being patient and measured instead of resorting to brow-beating or name-calling (**Proverbs 25:15**), you can have great success with those in authority that may not otherwise have been willing to take the "high road" of integrity.

Being Christ's faithful ambassador is never a liability, it is freeing to be able to do what is right and to know the Lord will bless your labors (**Romans 12:21**). That blessing may not be exactly what you were trying to accomplish, but it will yield fruit that will not perish but will instead have an everlasting impact.

RELYING ON HOPE AND A MIRACLE IS NOT A GOOD POLITICAL STRATEGY

"Whoever works his land will have plenty of bread,
but he who follows worthless pursuits lacks sense"
Proverbs 12:11

I t's exhilarating to run for political office. But excitement, though necessary, is not sufficient.

It's important to believe you have something to offer, that you have answers for how the government can work better, and that you can actually make a difference. And, you probably believe that people will recognize that you're the right person for the job when they find out about you.

As a believer, you have hopefully spent many hours in prayer (**1 Thessalonians 5:17**) and also sought good counsel before throwing your hat in the proverbial ring (**Luke 14:31**). You also know that a campaign is not just a game, it is mental, emotional and yes, spiritual combat. Because of that, sincerely seeking God's will and His wisdom is absolutely essential (**Romans 12:2; James 1:5**).

Now do a gut check. You may be the absolute best person to occupy that office, and everyone should be able to immediately recognize that. But history (and Scripture) shows that anything worthwhile will take a lot of "blood, sweat, and tears." Fields left to themselves are immediately overgrown with weeds (**Proverbs 24:30-34**). Children left to raise themselves will probably grow up with all sorts of issues (**Proverbs 29:15; Ephesians 6:4**). For any startup business to succeed, it will take a massive investment in time and energy (**Proverbs 10:4**). And every athlete knows it takes self-discipline and a lot of hard work to successfully compete (**1 Corinthians 9:24-27**).

Political campaigns consume enormous amounts of time, energy, resources, and commitment. To think that you can simply entrust the campaign into the Lord's hands and expect Him to bring about an election miracle is not just foolish, it's presumption towards God (**Proverbs 27:1; 1 Corinthians 10:9; James 2:14; 4:13-16**). It also treats lightly the efforts of any volunteers or financial donors you may have. This type of attitude is what **Romans 12:3** is referring to: thinking of yourself more highly than you ought.

Now, what about those supporting your campaign? Always be grateful for the volunteers that walk precincts, write letters, talk to others about you, and give financially to help you out. They are a real treasure. But, the more you rely on God to do all the work through them, while you just trust in the Lord, the less value you'll place on their sacrifices.

There are some, however, that will pray for you but will be unwilling or unable to do anything else. Be careful you don't resent those "volunteers." They're doing an important ministry by entering the Lord's throne room and interceding on your behalf. Sincere prayer is worth far more than gold (**James 5:17-18**), and having a group of prayer warriors should be a real encouragement to you and an incentive to do everything you can to honor their dedicated labors.

As in all of life, we value what we invest ourselves in. The more we put into something, the more it becomes dear to us. Just like valuing Jesus' death on the cross, the less we think we need sins forgiven, the less we make of Christ's death. The more we understand our need, the more our love of our Lord will grow.

Don't get me wrong, it's important to have hope, but it can't be an excuse to end up relying on a miracle or the efforts of others to carry you across the finish line. You also need to be "all in."

PRINCIPLE #53

POLITICS IS LIKE THE GOSPEL, TO BE EFFECTIVE IT MUST BE DONE LOCALLY

"Let no one seek his own good, but the good of his neighbor"
1 Corinthians 10:24

A re you the type that's "all talk, and no action"? Do you delight in thinking big thoughts and contemplating the majestic scheme of things, but have difficulty relating to the average person (**Proverbs 18:2**)? If so, then maybe politics isn't for you.

The weighty matters of state are important, as are city-wide issues and lofty mandates, but the average person is concerned about their everyday life and what directly impacts them. Politics can't just be about noble causes (though they're important); it can't just be about what's possible if only everyone agreed with you. It's about whose ox is being gored (**Exodus 21:35-36**) and how things can be made right.

Just as the gospel is shared from the heart and communicated person-to-person, so the most effective political influence is at the grassroots level, person-to-person. Paul exemplifies this by becoming all things to all people, meeting them where they were (**1 Corinthians 9:19-23**) so that he "might win more of them."

So, understanding local issues, and meeting people where they are in their lives (i.e. Jesus' example in **John 4:1-42**) is a powerful way to win them over. But just as the credibility of the gospel is affected by your credibility (although the gospel is spiritual and not dependent on human performance, see **Isaiah 55:10-11; Philippians 1:15-18**), your attempts to influence others must be sincere and not duplicitous like those of Absalom against David (**2 Samuel 15:1-6**).

Matthew 22:39 says to "love your neighbor as yourself"; it doesn't say to "love the world as yourself" or to delegate outreach to others that are more suited to do the work. In other words, you can't be the "trained professional" doing the strategic stuff, while the lowly volunteers are doing all the menial door-to-door stuff. Your personal touch, being done at the same level as the ones you want and need to connect to (i.e. the voters, the donors, the neighbors, etc.), will always be crucial.

Are you willing to make yourself vulnerable, or do you just want to stay aloof and be above it all? Are you too important to sink to doing lowly jobs? The disciples went from home-to-home and town-to-town (**Mark 6:7-11; Luke 9:2-5**) and didn't rely on some Galilee Gazette to proclaim their message.

Grand ideas and movements may influence many people for a short time, but the personal touch will affect the average person for a much longer time. This is true whether you're asking for a person's vote, for donations, for endorsements, for precinct walkers, for prayer, or for whatever else is needed.

The bottom line: one way or another, all politics is local. If you lose that perspective, you lose it at your own peril.

Part 10:
Putting Up With Christians

In politics, there is a built-in incentive to maintain a good working relationship with as many people as possible in order to further political goals. For Christians, however, there are imperatives that transcend mere pragmatics: we are to love one-another, defer to each other over less important matters, overlook weaknesses, and work together in an understanding way. Remember, we answer to our Lord for how we treat each other in this life; and that treatment is a testimony to the world of who we are in Christ.

Principle #54

In Essentials – Unity
In Non-Essentials – Liberty
In All Things – Charity

Ephesians 4:11-16; 5:15,20-21

I f Christians, rightfully or wrongly, differ over things like secondary doctrinal points, the application of biblical principles to life problems, what church music is most appropriate, and even what church government should look like, it's obvious they'll differ over political issues.

But political battles are a particularly difficult problem area because sincere believers vary so much in their understanding of a Christian's role, and so few actually hold anything resembling a biblical worldview. Given the intense hostility modern-day politics evokes, the potential for ungodly conflict throughout the church is high. Clearly, this situation is at odds with the unity the Lord desires for the body of Christ (**Psalm 133:1; 1 Corinthians 1:10; Ephesians 4:1-3**).

So, are there any essential political goals that believers can be united over? Several quickly come to mind: the sanctity of human life from conception to natural death (**Genesis 9:6; Exodus 20:13**), legitimate marriage being only one man and one woman for life (**Matthew 19:3-6**), the authority of parents to raise and educate their children (**Deuteronomy 6:4-9; Proverbs 22:6**), and the freedom of religious conscience (**Acts 5:29**). If a self-identified Christian disagrees over these, then they probably have a deeper problem with their understanding of God's Word.

Beyond the key issues above, there are hundreds more that believers may have conflicting views on because of personal experience, different depths of knowledge, and even a different understanding of the application of

Scripture. Think about gun control, climate change, protection of endangered species, capitalism, air and water quality thresholds, immigration, national threats, property taxes, refugees, and pandemic edicts. These are all complex and need to be looked at through the lens of Scripture if there's to be any possibility of agreement on how to approach them in a way that will honor the Lord.

But even after research, biblical study, prayer, and challenging each other (**Proverbs 27:17**) there may still be areas that escape complete unity. When that happens with a non-essential issue, it's important to remember that the Lord gives us the liberty to act according to our conscience (**Romans 14:1; Galatians 5:13**), but we are not to do that out of any self-interest (**Philippians 2:3-5**).

Political battles can be rough and tumble, but the more united believers can be in pursuing godly solutions to local, regional and national problems, the greater the opportunity to be successful in actually implementing effective solutions. However, the more divided believers are, the greater the opportunity for secular worldviews to control the narrative and implement disastrous solutions that ignore reality.

Like it or not, hotly contested political battles will continue until the Lord returns (**2 Peter 3:3-4**). In the meantime, you should always strive to live in an understanding way with your brothers and sisters, be wise in respecting each other's liberty to decide difficult problems according to the dictates of their conscience (particularly for non-essential issues), and always remain teachable yourself, knowing the Lord is ultimately the One that determines our steps (**Proverbs 13:18; 16:9**).

And finally, whether there is complete agreement or not, always be charitable about the motives of someone else (**1 Peter 4:8**). Defer to others whenever you can, knowing that we all will give an account to God for our decisions and our actions (**Romans 14:12, Hebrews 4:12-13**).

PRINCIPLE #55

WHEN DISAGREEMENTS OCCUR, WORK TO BE ABLE TO SPEAK WELL OF EACH OTHER

"Love is patient and kind; love does not envy or boast;
it is not arrogant or rude. It does not insist on its own way;
it is not irritable or resentful, it does not rejoice at wrong doing,
but rejoices with the truth"
1 Corinthians 13:4-6

You know the imperative, Jesus said "love one another" just as He has loved us (**John 15:12**). That's a tall order, particularly if you think you're clearly right about something, and the other person just doesn't get it. This can happen in families, with friends, at work, and yes with other believers laboring with you in the political realm.

One of the problems for any believer that is passionate about political work is that you can develop a morally superior attitude. Being convinced you have God's truth behind you, you start to claim the noble high ground and view any opposition as ignorant, misguided, or worse yet: evil. But what happens when a believer, using the same Bible, comes to a different position on a candidate, or policy, or piece of legislation?

If someone rejects the clear teachings of Scripture concerning life, marriage, and sexual purity, then there's merit to question what standard they are using to come to their positions. But there are other issues that reasonable people may sincerely differ on, such as immigration, gun control, or the homeless. So, what do you do when a dear brother or sister in the Lord has a personal conviction (**Romans 14:1-4,23b**) that differs from yours on a matter of public interest or even how to vote?

It's very tempting to do what the world would do: become wary of the other person, disparage them when you talk with others, refuse to have anything to do with them, or even give an appearance of respect but in your heart think of them as "damaged goods." All of these reactions are sinful and need to be recognized for what they are; a reflection of a judgmental spirit that emanates from pride (**Matthew 7:1-5; James 4:11-12**).

The Lord commands that we be longsuffering with each other, and show mutual respect (**Ephesians 4:1-3**). This isn't a conditional imperative dependent upon someone always agreeing with you. It is treating the other person with the dignity they have because they are also a child of God. Remember, they are adopted into the same family of God that you are (**Ephesians 1:3-6**) and like you, they will stand before the throne of Grace (**Romans 14:10-12**).

Instead of taking these disagreements personally and becoming defensive, wouldn't it be better to let them pass and concentrate on what you have in common? Wouldn't it be better, and more freeing, to speak well of the other person and be an encouragement to them instead of questioning their motives or thinking they are somehow now less worthy? In fact, wouldn't it be more Christ-honoring to acknowledge that you still have a lot to learn (**Proverbs 9:9; 13:18**) and you appreciate the other person's commitment to doing what is right, even though you may have some small differences between you?

Scripture is very clear; you're to think of the other person more highly than yourself (**Philippians 2:3**), rather than thinking in terms of them being for you or against you. Recognize that matters of conscience are non-trivial matters. So, as you have the opportunity, esteem your brother or sister, and you will have won a committed friend that will help you wherever and whenever they can (**Proverbs 27:10**).

PRINCIPLE #56

DIFFERENT PEOPLE SOLVE PROBLEMS IN DIFFERENT WAYS

"Who are you to pass judgment on the servant of another? It is before his own master that he stands or falls. And he will be upheld, for the Lord is able to make him stand"
Romans 14:4

People are obviously gifted in different ways (**1 Corinthians 12:4-7,14-20**). This includes how problems are defined and then solved. One person may take a very pragmatic approach, quickly look at advantages and disadvantages, make a decision that appears reasonable, and then move on with a willingness to adapt over time (**Proverbs 3:6**). Another person may examine the same problem in excruciating detail, gather as much information (data) as possible, look at weighted tradeoffs of different approaches, reassess potential solutions based on any new information, then determine the "best" decision possible and periodically redo the analysis completely (**Proverbs 24:27**).

The pragmatic person above could be giving great weight to being a good steward of people's time, relying on related experience, and then being willing to accept what could be a less-than-perfect answer to a problem. The detailed person can be driven by a need to find the "optimal" solution given all the variables involved, even if it takes significant time to find it. Both could very well be trusting in the Lord to ensure they're doing what's right (**Proverbs 19:21**).

When both types of problem solvers come up with the same answer, all is good. However, in so many political activities (i.e., campaigns) there are hundreds of major decisions that are needed to be made while racing against the election (or legislative session) clock.

For whichever description above may best describe you, some things must not be given up: doing what's right morally, ethically and legally, and not just being expeditious (**Psalm 32:8; Proverbs 16:3**).

So, can these two types of approaches be leveraged in a way that creates unity and not divisiveness? A reasonable approach would be to avoid the opportunity for conflict by having non-overlapping assignments.

The gifted detail person can work on items of high importance that must be done correctly, and where there's time to do an adequate analysis. These could be legal or financial issues, official documentation, and identification of high-impact, long-range strategies. It could also be critical areas that have a very high risk associated with them, and there's adequate time to do a "deep dive" analysis. Generally, they're not the person for a complicated, nuanced (or "fuzzy") problem requiring a quick decision.

The gifted pragmatic person is needed to address the quick reaction types of problems that are generally less conducive to detailed analysis. By their nature, these types of problems will probably have to depend heavily on experience and intuition. Examples would include: personnel assignments, messaging to a broad audience, sensitive negotiations that are affected by conflicting personal motivations and desires, etc.

The key is for both problem solvers to have regard for the other's abilities (**Proverbs 22:29**), to encourage each other (**1 Thessalonians 5:11**), and to not bind the other's conscience (**Romans 14:4**).

Incidentally, there's a third type of "problem solver," the one that cannot make a decision for fear of making the wrong decision (**Proverbs 22:13**). It's not that this person can't be productive and do useful work; it's that they shouldn't be put in any leadership position that requires making decisions affecting others. There are plenty of tasks that can be done; they just need to be tasks that are tailored to this person's strengths.

Part 11:
Dealing With Non-Christians

Purely political circles, campaigns and events are rarely populated only by Christians. Politics by its nature involves working with or influencing a wide range of people, with many not necessarily sharing your commitment to Christ. So, whatever the venue, whatever the goal, you need to know what you are talking about, how to work with those that may have a different view of morality or ultimate accountability, and also how to ensure your witness for Christ is not compromised.

PRINCIPLE #57
BUMPER STICKERS WON'T WIN THE DAY

"If the iron is blunt, and one does not sharpen the edge,
he must use more strength, but wisdom helps one to succeed"
Ecclesiastes 10:10

I t's fun to have a clever little phrase that encapsulates truth, and then spring it on others when needed. Catch phrases are a bullet in the arsenal of political warfare and are used by both sides. They typically contain a kernel of truth, and can often be embedded with sarcasm that is meant to shut down any further conversation. Typically, they are meant to give the appearance of saying something profound when there's very little time available (like when leaving an elevator).

Although pithy statements serve a purpose, they probably won't carry the day to convince others of the rightness of your views. Most issues of the day are far more complicated than simple one-liners can encapsulate. And, truth be told, many times a slogan actually can draw attention away from the real substance of the concern at hand. But useful or not, it's critical that you understand the major factors around a public concern so that if pressed you can articulate what you stand for and why (i.e., the weighty "stuff" behind the statement).

This is part of what the apostle Paul was referring to when he said it's good to have zeal, but not without knowledge (**Romans 10:2**). You need to be a person of substance, not just a source of catch-phrases (**Proverbs 18:13**). Politicians often rely on repeating short, emotionally charged claims (like referring to someone as a racist) whether there's any proof to support that accusation or not (**Proverbs 26:11**). But zealously denigrating someone without substantial, unambiguous evidence to back it up is wickedness

(**Proverbs 24:8-9**), whether it's effective with those that are just plain gullible, or not (**Proverbs 29:8**).

So, what's a person to do? First, be knowledgeable about both sides of a major issue, and not just your key bullet points. For skeptical (but not hostile) groups, try to find some common ground to emphasize. This will give you credibility and a possible opening for more detailed discussions. It will also help to ensure you aren't talking past each other and never really "communicating" with each other.

Secondly, know your audience. Those that are just trying to embarrass you or create a "gotcha" moment are not worth engaging. They only intend harm and are probably not going to be teachable or listen to anything you have to say (**Proverbs 26:4; 29:9**). Only rarely will you be able to successfully respond in a manner that exposes their duplicity and carries your message well (**Proverbs 26:5**). For those cases, a short, clever phrase may be all you want to use, and then move on.

If you're being formally interviewed (newspaper, radio, TV, or group setting), remember that the longer the interview the greater the opportunity to say something that can be taken out of context. This is one reason why polished public speakers stay "on point" and keep circling back to their main points while giving a little more substance each time. This approach prevents going down rabbit trails or saying something off the cuff that isn't relevant to their position (**Proverbs 10:19**).

Finally, relying on bromides can suffer from what Scripture describes as using a blunt tool (**Ecclesiastes 10:10**). If that's all you have in your repertoire, then raising your voice, or shouting, or showing great emotion is all you have to make your point more forceful, instead of drawing from a depth of reasoned understanding. This type of emotional outburst is what characterizes much of what "useful idiots" are seen doing on the evening news when some event is being protested. Emotion (zeal) can be good, but substance (knowledge) is equal if not more important (**Proverbs 29:11; Ecclesiastes 9:17**).

YOU CAN HAVE COMMON CAUSE
WITHOUT BECOMING UNEQUALLY "YOKED"

"Do not be unequally yoked with unbelievers.
For what partnership has righteousness with lawlessness?
Or what fellowship has light with darkness?"
2 Corinthians 6:14

Most political campaigns or legislative activists are eager to curry the help of as many different people and organizations as possible. It not only shows a broad spectrum of support, but sheer numbers help ensure a ballot or lobbying success. The usual standard for acceptance is anybody, except for those that would bring public condemnation your way (i.e., anarchist groups, the KKK, skin heads, extreme religious cults, and others considered far out of line with acceptable beliefs or practices).

For a Christian, there's another concern. Reliance on, or working with unbelievers that may share your same political goal, but don't share the same respect for Jesus Christ or His Word. Put a different way: may a Christian work cooperatively with, for example, an atheist? Does "cooperation" mean you are in some way compromising your faith, or violating the principles in **2 Corinthians 6:14** about being unequally yoked?

To most believers, this isn't a hard question. As long as you don't have to deny Jesus Christ or your fundamental beliefs, you're free to work together politically. Paul worked as a tentmaker (**Acts 18:1-3**), undoubtedly helping many non-believers prosper. He also pointed out we work and live in a sinful world and often associate with the ungodly in daily life as we exemplify Christ in our lives (**1 Corinthians 5:9-10**). Paul even appealed to ungodly, idolatrous government officials for justice (**Acts**

25:8-12). Jesus Himself reflected this reality as He befriended sinners (**Matthew 9:10-13**) to witness to them.

But for some Christians, working with those who clearly reject Jesus Christ may be a difficult conscience issue on multiple levels. For one, you could be so sensitive to ensuring everything's done in a pure manner by everyone involved that you become a hindrance to anything getting done at all.

Another concern you could have is giving the appearance of compromise to other believers by working with politically driven unbelievers. In reality, these are opportunities for you to not only exemplify Christ to unbelievers, but to explain to believers the nature of your freedom in Christ (**Galatians 5:13**) to serve the common good, while still not compromising your beliefs.

The real issue is whether a political position, statement, or binding document clearly presents something you cannot agree with. This can occur with joint statements written to show united support from a range of religious and secular factions. When this happens, the gospel may be watered down, misrepresented or even wrongly described to obtain a more "unifying" faith community message of support. The same difficulty can occur if you're asked to concur with or participate in a political tactic that's clearly immoral. In both these cases, there's a "yoking" of sorts that binds you to an unacceptable action that requires you to support and defend it. These are the times to politely but firmly reject an opportunity to lend credibility to what is obviously wrong.

If these types of issues come up as part of your campaign, you have lots of control over what you'll allow to happen. If you're part of someone else's campaign or lobbying activities, you need to decide whether these (or less obvious) decisions negatively reflect on you and your witness to others. If they do, your continuing role may have to come to an end in order to honor the Lord.

These can be tough decisions, but remember God's common grace can still allow a lot of common ground with those in the world in order to accomplish good for everyone's benefit.

Principle #59

Pursuing Politics Assists The Proclamation Of The Gospel

"But seek the welfare of the city where I have sent you into exile,
and pray to the Lord on its behalf,
for in its welfare you will find your welfare"
Jeremiah 29:7

As a Christian, you have a heartfelt concern for those who don't know Jesus Christ as their Lord and Savior. You know that eternity waits for us all, and so you have a justifiable concern for a nonbeliever's destiny without Christ. You also know you have been given the imperative to share Christ since believers are His chosen spokesmen in this world (**Matthew 28:18-20; Romans 10:14-17**).

So, does it mean that sharing the gospel must be put on the back burner until some later time to minimize the risk of unnecessarily offending someone you need to work with (**1 Corinthians 2:14; 10:31-33**)? Does being politically motivated mean, you're not actively promulgating the gospel? The obvious answer is "No" for several reasons.

The first is that working to restrain the government from becoming hostile to your beliefs helps to ensure proclaiming the gospel is not restrained. If unchecked, the government can and will be used against believers by those that despise our values and God's truths. After all, governments are instituted by God to help create an environment for the growth of good (**Romans 13:3-4**), and that includes protecting what our nation was founded on: the concept of freedom of religious conscience in an individual's and a church's public and private activities.

The second is your personal example. As you make decisions concerning your political aspirations, or who to support, you're giving a first-hand testimony of what's important in your life. You demonstrate that you answer to a higher authority by submitting to the Lordship of Jesus Christ. By not practicing the ungodly ways of the world (lying, deceit, misrepresentation, character assassination, intimidation, etc.) you show the quality of your character and that leading a holy life is far more important than "winning" at all costs.

Also, more often than not people will quickly know if you're a Christian. You won't talk like others, you won't tell or listen to "dirty" jokes (**Ephesians 5:3-4**), and you won't stab people in the back or gossip. In fact, because there really is something different about you, they'll be sensitive to anything you may say or do that runs counter to what they think Christians should be like. Knowing this alone will help keep you on the "straight and narrow."

Your example is important for another reason. It will bring glory to God (**1 Peter 2:12**) in ways you never imagined and will be blessed by God as He puts to shame those who don't like you (**1 Peter 3:13-17**). On the other hand, a bad example could bring discredit on other believers running for office by giving ammunition to those that are hostile to anything Christian.

Finally, the Lord will provide opportunities to share the gospel. When and where will be a wisdom issue, so praying for those you'll be working with is an important spiritual discipline to cultivate. Even Paul proclaimed gospel truth to Agrippa the king (**Acts 26:1-29**), and in Macedonia (**Acts 16:9-10**), yet didn't in Asia and Bithynia (**Acts 16:6-7**). Jesus prevented others from talking about Him at times (**Mark 1:40-44; 5:35-43**), while at other times He said to do so (**Mark 5:14-20**). The Lord will show you the proper times and circumstances!

You know you're the aroma of Christ. To believers you're the aroma of life and to those that are perishing you're the aroma of death (**2 Corinthians 2:15-16**). Remember, this is all by the Lord's doing so that by your "good works" (and example) your Heavenly Father will be glorified (**Matthew 5:16**).

PART 12:
POLITICAL WARFARE IS NOT FOR THE TIMID

Political battles are now openly disruptive, divisive and destructive in our nation. After society's long, generational slide towards moral relativism and the growth of an all-powerful, over-reaching government, our nation is no longer inching towards socialism (Marxism) but is actively embracing it. Spiritual wickedness takes no prisoners, and when given power it will never give it back. So, the question really is: are you up for the fight? Are you willing to invest the time and energy needed to be godly salt and light in the political arena for the sake of the gospel? As you read these last chapters, ask yourself: what would the Lord want you to do?

NEVER UNDERESTIMATE THE WICKEDNESS OF SECULAR OPPOSITION

"Be sober-minded; be watchful. Your adversary the devil prowls around like a roaring lion, seeking someone to devour"
1 Peter 5:8

B ig shocker: political secularists do not play by the rules. The ideology they live by is to win at all costs. Does this mean no one on their side has any integrity or sincerely wants to make a difference for the common good? Of course not! But the worldview behind secular humanism is that there is no God, Christianity is both stupid and dangerous, and man defines what truth is.

Is there any doubt then, why hypocrisy isn't very shameful to a pure secularist, that facts (and reality) and open debate and reasoned discourse are often rejected as a means to approach public policy and laws, and that any means appears to be justified to gain some theoretically noble end?

If a political ideology and worldview can celebrate: abortion for any or no reason at all, passive and active euthanasia, physician-assisted suicide, research using embryonic stem cells and aborted baby parts, and has more empathy for an endangered weed than for life created in God's image (**Genesis 1:26-27**), then how can this political movement be trusted with power? For anyone with a conscience, these life-destroying ends should be inviting disgust and revulsion. But wait, there's more.

If consciences are seared (or incredibly misled), it's not surprising that anything confronting such wickedness will be fought "tooth and nail." Faithless, political secularists are masters at dismissing, denigrating, and destroying anyone that opposes them. Whether it's matters of life, family, sexual purity, freedom of religious conscience, or even education, they revel in publically promoting evil as good, and defining what God calls good as being something that's evil (**Isaiah 5:20-21**). They also seem unable or unwilling to objectively look at the destructiveness of their "beliefs" (**1 Corinthians 2:14; 2 Corinthians 4:3-4**). This form of blindness can only be understood from a spiritual perspective. So, where's the source of this ideology and breathtaking blindness?

Scripture is clear that Satan has been a liar and murderer since the very beginning (**John 8:43-44**). The description of Satan as a roaring lion prowling around to devour someone is not just a literary illustration (**1 Peter 5:8**); it's a profound warning about how dangerous Satan really is. If he's bold enough to directly challenge Jesus Christ (**Matthew 4:1-11**), what is he going to do with human pawns (or "useful idiots") open to lies that appeal to flawed human reason instead of God's truth (**Proverbs 16:25**)?

Is it any wonder that a wicked creature (and those spiritual beings in league with him) that can appear as an angel of light (**2 Corinthians 11:14**) wouldn't try to convince as many people as possible that wickedness is righteousness and that true righteousness must be maligned and completely destroyed (**2 Timothy 4:3-4**)?

If you ignore or misunderstand the nature of this political threat, it will be at your personal peril. On your own, you will be helpless to withstand the onslaught of smooth talk and deceptive lies that come from self-righteous and miss-guided people; whether from politicians, the liberal news media, academia, social media, Hollywood, or any other source of influence. But the good news is that the Lord will give you what you need to resist the Devil (**1 Peter 5:9**), and to stand for what is right (**Matthew 10:16-22**).

The bottom line is to test everything, keep what is good, and reject every form of evil (**1 Thessalonians 5:21-22**). Honor the Lord in all that you do and you will be blessed (**John 12:26**) and strengthened by Him (**2 Corinthians 12:8-10**).

Principle #61

It's Not "Right Versus Left"
It's "Good Versus Evil"

"For we do not wrestle against flesh and blood,
but against the rulers, against the authorities, against the
cosmic powers over this present darkness, against the
spiritual forces of evil in the heavenly places"
Ephesians 6:12

A t a very basic level, political warfare is merely a reflection of the ongoing warfare between light (**John 8:12**) and darkness (**John 3:20**), and between life (**John 14:6**) and death (**John 8:44**). In our day, the broad-spectrum of political views has been generalized with the secular terms "right" versus "left," with extremes and moderates as variations on both sides. To the uninitiated, these political terms may imply some moral equivalency, with each just promoting a competing view of the nature of truth, life, sexuality, family, justice, the role of government, and who or what we're ultimately accountable to, if anything.

The reality, however, is that there's a fundamental difference between right and left in our nation; and those differences have both temporal and eternal consequences. The core ideology of the "left" generally embraces an ever-evolving definition of truth and believes that mankind's reasoning is the ultimate measure of everything. By believing it holds the moral high ground, the left feels justified to condemn any opposition as being evil. The philosophical underpinnings of the "right" generally subscribe to God's transcendent truths about the nature of the world, its institutions, the nature of mankind, and our ultimate accountability to a just and holy God. This is the "right" that God refers to in **Ecclesiastes 10:2**, as opposed to the foolishness of the natural man's heart that inclines to the metaphorical "left."

Although "left" and "right" are convenient political constructs, God's Word establishes truth about reality. In fact, God's Word is the measure against which everything is to be compared. That's what **Proverbs 4:27** is talking about when it says to not stray off the path to either "the right or the left" (that is: life decisions, not political leanings) because doing so will lead to evil. Jesus relates the same concept in **Matthew 7:13-14**.

What does this have to do with you? Actually, a lot!

The political reality in our nation is that there are two dominant political parties, one of which (the "right") is more closely aligned with a more comprehensive understanding of the principles of God's Word than the other. With Scripture as the basis, conservative political values and goals can be derived as a natural result. The closer these values align with God's truth, the greater the blessings for a person and a nation (**Deuteronomy 28:1-67**). God's Word always leads to abundant life, while a man-centered worldview will only lead to disaster (**John 10:10, Colossians 2:8**) if it ignores reality and trusts in politicians instead of a holy God.

As these political realities play out, it really is a battle between good (politics as it conforms to God's truths) and evil (politics that reject God's truths).

Are there individual exceptions within the "left"? Of course! Is the "right" without blemish? Of course not! But if someone thinks they are doing "good" by buying into the dominantly secular worldview and goals of the "left" they are either naïve, willfully ignorant, or insensitive to the inevitably dangerous consequences that result when secular progressives gain control of governmental power.

Spiritual warfare is serious business, and the open political warfare underway around us is a war over our nation's soul (**Proverbs 29:2**). When a political worldview is consistent with the Prince of Darkness (**John 8:44; Ephesians 6:12**) and not the Prince of Peace (**Isaiah 9:6; John 14:27**), we should do everything we can to prevent that worldview from gaining any political power.

PRINCIPLE #62

IF YOU'RE NOT BEING ATTACKED, YOU'RE PROBABLY NOT IN THE BATTLE

"If you faint in the day of adversity, your strength is small"
Proverbs 24:10

Which would you rather be: a warrior (**Ephesians 6:10**) or a coward (**Proverbs 22:13; 26:13**)?

As a Christian, you know spiritual conflict is going on all around you. Why else would Paul give such clear warnings about it (**Ephesians 6:10-12**), and say you need to be equipped for battle (**Ephesians 6:13-18**).

Jesus resisted attacks by the Devil (**Matthew 4:1-11**) and was eventually murdered (**John 19:1-30**); Paul suffered greatly for the gospel (**2 Corinthians 11:23-29**); Peter was beaten by the religious authorities (**Acts 5:27-41**); and Christians continue to be tortured, disenfranchised, even murdered around the world because of their faith (**1 Peter 4:12-19**).

Living by your convictions is not just sitting back and intellectually analyzing the battles around you and applying nuanced theological arguments. It's rolling up your sleeves and getting involved with the messiness of politics and political combat.

Ask yourself this question; are you willing to "stand in the breach" (**Ezekiel 22:30**), and work hard to restrain governments to their proper biblical functions of executing justice and encouraging good? Are you willing to be a "watchman" for the Lord (**Ezekiel 33:1-6**) to prevent the continuing erosion of our religious freedom to proclaim God's Word and live by the dictates of our conscience in public as well as in our private lives?

The easier path is to "go along to get along" with the world. Consider the ten spies that came back from spying out the Promised Land that were cowards and turned God's people against what God commanded them to do (**Numbers 13:1-14:10**). Joshua and Caleb, however, were courageous warriors and knew what needed to be done (**Numbers 14:6-9**). The former spies were cursed, the latter were blessed.

Ultimately, what are you afraid of? If God is for you who can prevail against you (**Romans 8:35-39**)? If your concerns revolve around being "Friended" or "Unfriended" on Facebook, or your battles amount to a back-and-forth war of words on Twitter, then maybe you're not a Joshua or Caleb and politics isn't for you. We know that God culled out those that were faint of heart or that couldn't be trusted to be part of Gideon's "army" (**Judges 7:3**). So, what do you want to be: a leader, someone enthusiastically supporting a leader, or just an observer?

If you choose the easy path (**Matthew 7:13-14**), remember, Satan prowls around for someone to devour (**1 Peter 5:8**). That description is one of action and initiative in seeking you out to harm you. You're not going to be able to hide indefinitely or sit back and just let others do the hard work. **Second Timothy 4:7** gives us the example of Paul running the race to completion, fighting the good fight. Is that going to be you or not?

Living a Christian life, no matter what you're involved in, will be a challenge. There will always be difficulties to face, hard decisions to make, and plenty of opportunities to grow in sanctification. But in politics, maybe more so than in most other pursuits, you'll be attacked with or without justification personally and professionally. In fact, the more prominent you become, the more influential you are, the more vicious the political/spiritual battle will become.

So, are you a warrior? If not, do you want to be a warrior? Do you want to receive the crown of life promised to those that remain steadfast under trial (**James 1:12**)? If so, study hard, work hard, get involved, and trust in the Lord (**Proverbs 3:5-6**).

Principle #63

If You Aren't In The Political Battle, Are You Being True To Your Faith?

"So also faith by itself, if it does not have works, is dead"
James 2:17

Politics isn't for everyone. That being said, if you cast a vote (or don't vote) you're making a political statement. Every time you comment about a politician, or complain about a law, or a family dispute over illegal immigration breaks out – politics is the backdrop. Like it or not, everyone participates in politics to some degree. Even if you never discuss anything controversial, never vote, never express a political preference of any kind – you're giving the impression that politics is not worth your time or attention; that's a political statement.

The fact you are reading this booklet shows you have more than just a passing interest in politics. Maybe you've thought about contributing financially to a political cause or campaign; maybe you've been asked to walk precincts or stuff envelopes or participate in a phone bank for a candidate, but haven't ever done it. Maybe you've even thought about running for elective office, but don't feel qualified or don't have the initiative to figure out if that's right for you. All of these activities are good, but are you doing them? And if you're not doing anything, why aren't you?

The very nature of faith is putting our trust in a God that loves us (**Proverbs 3:5-6; John 3:16**) and has good works for us to do (**Ephesians 2:10**). Those works include proclaiming the gospel (**Matthew 28:18-20**), helping those in need (**Matthew 22:39**), and being salt and light (**Matthew 5:13-16**), all for the glory of God (**1 Corinthians 10:31**).

But, objectively speaking, what's the greatest danger in our country to the proclamation of the gospel? It's any government that's hostile to our convictions and that allows unrestrained high-tech "cancel culture" to censor our free speech. It's any government that implements wicked anti-life, anti-marriage, and anti-sexual purity values on the entire nation through public policy and public education. It's any government that has used its immense power to cripple the influence of Christ-honoring organizations and people that stand for truth. And, it's any government that can no longer be trusted to objectively tell the truth to its citizens.

Given the ever increasing threats to our right to exercise our freedom of religion, is it so difficult to see that every major political battle ultimately relates to the gospel one way or the other? If the connection is hard to see, then you may need a gut check on what it means to be salt and light. After all, our system of governance asks its citizenry who should make the laws of the land, what is the evil to be punished, and what is the good that's to be commended (**Romans 13:3-4**). Your involvement in making these decisions is a political decision that will have an impact on your Christian witness and ultimately our religious freedoms.

Exercising your faith will also lead to taking the initiative to call out evil for what it is (**Ephesians 5:11**), the initiative to be a godly influence in the darkened recesses of otherwise unchecked political hegemony (**Matthew 5:13-16**), and the initiative to become educated in the issues of the day and how God's Word applies (**Romans 12:2**).

The bottom line is that an ambassador is not to be weak and ineffective in defending the interests of the kingdom they are to represent (**2 Corinthians 5:20; 1 Peter 2:9**). God's ambassador doesn't just let the family of God be maligned, misrepresented, or destroyed. Instead, ambassadors represent their kingdom's interests accurately and boldly, and show how the way of the King of kings, and Lord of lords is best for the common good, and how it ultimately will bring glory to God.

You belong to Christ, and you are one of His ambassadors!

YOU'RE TO BE FAITHFUL, BUT YOU CANNOT GUARANTEE RESULTS

"Again I saw that under the sun the race is not to the swift,
nor the battle to the strong, nor bread to the wise,
nor riches to the intelligent, nor favor to those with knowledge,
but time and chance happen to them all"
Ecclesiastes 9:11

Warfare of any kind is not pretty. Political warfare in our nation is typically non-violent, but there are life and death consequences (i.e. victims) that result from our national, state, and local governmental decisions. Think of the loss of life through abortion, the impact of defunding the police, allowing open borders that encourage drug and child trafficking, and funding of social programs that incentivize broken families and generational dependence on the government.

Your interest and involvement in politics is a serious matter with serious consequences. Since any political activity can easily breed conflict of some kind, good planning is critical and biblical (**Proverbs 21:5; Luke 14:28-33**). But, just like most of life's more difficult adventures, things will change all the time (**Ecclesiastes 9:11**). Given that reality, it's important to keep the goal in focus, while not compromising on the methods used to get there (**Proverbs 16:9**). The key is to remain faithful to what needs to be done, while not becoming discouraged if the "goal" is not accomplished (e.g., an election campaign loss, a failed lobbying effort, loss of support for a new law or policy, etc.).

The fact of the matter is, no matter how hard you work, no matter how many resources are applied, no matter how much you pray, no matter how noble the cause, obtaining the goal may not happen. Even if you've done everything humanly possible, you cannot guarantee any specific result. If your personal worth is dependent upon "winning," you'll eventually become very disheartened and potentially even depressed. When important things don't turn out the way you wanted, you need to keep the following in mind.

First, the Apostle Paul didn't ask for the difficulties he encountered in his ministry labors (**2 Corinthians 11:23-33**), but through them he accomplished what the Lord wanted to have done (**Philippians 4:11-13**). Despite what most people would see as setbacks, Paul pleased the Lord by running the race to completion (**2 Timothy 4:7-8**).

Second, you must not let "winning" be the measure of you or your understanding of (or trust in) God's sovereignty. The Lord may have something else in mind that will fulfill His purposes, and your desires may not have aligned with them. Not having success may not be a bad thing; it could actually be opening the door for a better opportunity in the future. Either way, you shouldn't become anxious or discouraged since God is in ultimate control and will give you peace (**Philippians 4:6-7**).

Third, if you do find yourself becoming depressed, ask yourself if you are being presumptuous about what you expected God to do (**James 4:13-16**)? If you have been presuming, confess it and move on with whatever new lessons you've been able to learn. Remember, there will always be plenty of new battles waiting for you to engage in to honor the Lord (**1 Timothy 6:12a**).

Finally, you need to be continually in prayer asking for the Lord's help, His guidance, and for His will to be done (**Matthew 6:6; 18:19-20; John 15:7; Philippians 4:6**). As you pray, you'll undoubtedly have in mind what you think a godly outcome will be and what needs to be done to get there. But the more you try to limit the Lord, the harder the lessons you'll have to learn about how to conform to His will (**Romans 12:2; 1 John 5:13-15**). Instead, work hard, stay focused, always be flexible, but entrust the results into God's sovereign hands (**Proverbs 3:5-6; 1 Corinthians 3:6-7**).

Principle #65
Never Give Up

"Be strong and courageous. Do not fear or be in dread of them,
for it is the Lord your God who goes with you.
He will not leave you or forsake you"
Deuteronomy 31:6

"Do not be slothful in zeal, be fervent in spirit, serve the Lord"
Romans 12:11

The apostle Paul summarized his life well in **2 Timothy 4:7**: "I have fought the good fight, I have finished the race, I have kept the faith" (see also **Acts 20:24; 1 Corinthians 9:23-25; Hebrews 12:1-3**). Throughout your life, you're to pursue kingdom work until you're taken home to your heavenly abode (**John 14:1-3**). The retirement system for believers is eternal life; but until you're with the Lord you're to faithfully run the race He sets before you while here on earth.

If that race is in the political realm, then do it with the same enthusiasm you would any other important ministry area. But you must do it without sacrificing your family, your friends, your church, your integrity, and especially without bringing any dishonor to the name of Christ. You are not "in it to win it" at all costs or make political ambition an idol, but you are in it for the common good (**Matthew 5:13-16**), for the benefit of God's people, and for the glory of God (**1 Corinthians 10:31**).

If you are to lead, then lead while remaining accountable to those that are more mature in the Lord. If you are better suited to support other leaders, then support them vigorously in as many ways as possible. If you can provide wise counsel, insights or analysis, then do so with a clear conscience (**Psalm 119:105; Proverbs 11:14; 15:22; 20:18; 24:6**). Whatever your giftedness (**1 Corinthians 12:4-7**), and whatever the opportunities the Lord provides (**Ecclesiastes 11:6**), pursue them with fervor as long as you can (**Romans 12:11**).

Your engagement in the political realm will be greater or less depending on what phase of life you're in. But remember, you're doing this for the Lord, and for your family, and for the generations that follow since governments and political conflict will exist far longer than a single lifespan.

We know that the natural inclination of ungodly governance (**Proverbs 29:2**) is to eventually turn against God and everyone that belongs to Him (**Psalm 2:1-12**). So, could there be personal risk involved with political activism? Yes! But remember that with a few glaring exceptions, political battles in our nation are disruptive but typically not bloody. Because our Lord is merciful, we know your work to restore and then maintain righteousness in the public square will pay eternal dividends to countless others that may not have an opportunity to exert influence like you do (**Proverbs 24:10-12**). Political engagement is an important calling; a calling that once engaged will be difficult to walk away from.

So, whether you run for office, support a campaign, lobby for godly legislation, raise financial support, provide counsel to leaders, or whatever you do, do it well (**Colossians 3:23-24**), do it with zeal (**Romans 12:11**), do it without fear (**Romans 8:33-39**), and do it unto the Lord (**1 Corinthians 10:31**) with the strength that He provides (**Philippians 4:13**).

Finally, always remember that in serving the King of kings (**1 Timothy 6:15**) you are ultimately serving the gospel, knowing that no matter how wicked or misguided governments become, with your help they will never prevail against the Lord or His kingdom (**Matthew 16:18**).

ENDNOTE

You've been warned!

Being a Christian and wanting to "change the world" through political ministry is a difficult, but rewarding pursuit. I was "bit" by the politics bug over 25 years ago, and the interest has never gone away. And, I don't expect it to ever go away until I am taken home to my Heavenly Father.

Whether you are a "newbie" to this world, or a seasoned politician with many years under your belt, my prayer is that this book has challenged you. I also pray that it will stimulate some honest introspection about how you are going to invest yourself in this minefield in the days and years ahead.

While you consider that future, if you would like to share your personal experiences, or you want clarification on any of the material in this book, or if you disagree with something I have written, feel free to contact me any time. I can be reached by email at:

frankkacer@hotmail.com

To God be the glory!

In Christ's eternal love,
Frank Kacer

Jude 24,25

ABOUT THE AUTHOR

Frank Kacer has been a Christian worldview political activist for over twenty-five years. Besides authoring numerous columns for Christian publications and online with the *Washington Times "Communities"* and *Communities Digital News*; he has produced his unique *"Kacer's Call"* biblical perspective on every California statewide Proposition since 2002 and local Measures since 2010.

A frequent guest speaker at churches and conservative groups on political issues from a biblical perspective, Frank has been instrumental in advising many church-based salt-and-light and Christian citizenship ministries. As Founder and Executive Director of the Christian Citizenship Council (C3), Frank has a long history of mentoring Christians to engage in politics in a biblically balanced, Christ-honoring and legal manner. Since early 2019 Frank has also served as the Research, Content and Curriculum Director for Well Versed ministries, helping to bring biblical principles of governance directly to government leaders.

In the political realm, Frank has been elected to county Central Committee political office, been a state party delegate, and been active in political campaigns and strategic planning, candidate recruitment, get-out-the-vote activities, precinct operations and training of volunteers.

Professionally, Frank was a physicist in the Department of Defense Intelligence Community for over 35 years, and a senior systems engineer with Science Applications International Corporation (SAIC) for 12 years. He has a B.A. in Physics from Western Washington State College (now University) and a M.S. from U.C.L.A. in Engineering/Operations Research.

Frank and Lynn have been married since 1973, reside in San Diego California, and have three married children and five grandchildren. He has previously served as an elder at Grace Bible Church for over 28 years where he was responsible for outreach ministries, and currently serves in an emeritus status.